For Jason Rea,
With joy & hope in
the gospel!

Dave Caun

I Will Hold My Candle

And Other Stories for Christmas

Dave Carver

I Will Hold My Candle And Other Stories for Christmas

Copyright © 2011 By David B. Carver

ISBN 978-1-257-64661-6

The poem on p. 10, "In a Botticelli Print", is by Luci Shaw in *Listen To The Green* (Harold Shaw, 1971) p. 12. Used by permission of the author.

"Santa Claus And St. Nicholas" on p. 71 is used by permission of the authors, J. Rosenthal & C. Myers, The St. Nicholas Center www.stnicholascenter.org

<u>Illustrations:</u>
The line drawings throughout the book are courtesy of Ariel R. Carver.
Cover photo: Burning Candle, © Mariusz Szachowski | Dreamstime.com
Author photo courtesy Sharon M. Carver
The image on p. 61 is courtesy of dan / FreeDigitalPhotos.net
The image on p. 97, Red Bow, © Budda | Dreamstime.com

Contents

Forward: Why stories, anyway?

When I was a child, I really didn't like going to church. It was a somber, serious place, where grown-ups talked about important (and, to me, boring) things. We sang songs that had words in them like "fount" and "terrestrial" and "cherubim". It was, it seemed to me, all about being quiet and listening and making sure that I didn't embarrass anyone (especially my mother!). So most weeks, I did everything I could to avoid making the trip.

But there was one time when I loved going to church: Christmas Eve. Going to church at night was a lot of fun, and the grown-ups seemed to be a little more relaxed at the 11:00 p.m. service than they were in the morning, and there were a lot more people of all ages. The songs were all ones that I knew, and they even let us hold candles when we sang. But the best part about Christmas Eve for me was when our pastor, Mr. Wysham, got up to preach. Because instead of talking theology to the adults, he told us stories. Each year, as I recall, he gave us stories about Christmas – verbal images that allowed me to grasp the magic and mystery of the incarnation. Stories that excited my imagination and aroused my curiosity…stories that pointed to The Story.

And lo, it came to pass that in the succeeding years, I moved to the other side of the pulpit. Now, I am the one in charge of picking the music and I'm the one who talks theologically in long and, yes, sometimes boring sermons to the adults. Yet as Christmas Eve approaches each year, I find myself longing to express The Story in a new way. For twenty years, I have tried each year to write a story that will express some aspect of the mystery of the incarnation in ways that surprise and challenge listeners of every age. My thinking is that if there is one story that folks know from the Scripture, it's Christmas…and if those folks are not in church very often, they can be tempted to "tune out" the theologizing because they feel like they know the story already and what else is the pastor going to say after 2000 years of Shepherds and Wise Men and Angels?

But the Gospel – the good news – is always intrusive, always surprising. So in the stories I've written, I've attempted to show how that Good News can interrupt lives in a hundred different ways.

Some of these stories are written in the first person. That is strictly a literary device – they are not in any sense autobiographical (I mention this because one Christmas Eve an eight year old boy came out of church with his mother saying, "That was a good story, mom, but I still can't believe that Jesus was born in Pastor Dave's back yard!"). Some of these tales involve dreams and visions. You have those, too – and I hope that these accounts give you space to explore those areas of your spirit. A few of them, such as "I Will Hold My Candle" or "Dangerous Love" have their inspiration in an historical event. All of them are rooted, one way or another, in The Story as found in Scripture. My hope is that as you read them, you will remember that the Bible can be, for each of us, a letter, or a diary, or some other form of message from the Lord – the Lord who is not content to be aloof and removed from our lives, but who insists on interrupting our daily lives with His presence and his promise.

My hope is that sharing these stories will invite you to consider where and how the Lord is moving in the midst of your own life. My core belief is that stories have the deepest impact when we hear them aloud – so I would encourage you to speak these stories to yourself, or even better, to a couple of friends.

I am profoundly grateful to my wife, Sharon, and daughter, Ariel, who have given me space to birth these tales. In particular, Sharon has asked wonderful questions in October and November as I begin to wonder what the story will be in that particular year. I appreciate Stephanie, who for more than a decade has met with me on Christmas Eve morning to hear the story first, and who is a good editor and a better friend. My friend Casie, who has listened to my stories for more than half my life, took the drafts of some of these stories and pushed me to deepen the imagery and tighten the language. I delight in a congregation that seems to encourage this kind of playfulness from their pastor on a sacred evening, and I offer this collection as my gift to any kid who has ever been bored in church in the hopes that somehow, somewhere, a glimmer of God's love will shine through these words.

Luke 2:1-20

1In those days Caesar Augustus issued a decree that a census should be taken of the entire Roman world. 2(This was the first census that took place while Quirinius was governor of Syria.) 3And everyone went to his own town to register.

4So Joseph also went up from the town of Nazareth in Galilee to Judea, to Bethlehem the town of David, because he belonged to the house and line of David. 5He went there to register with Mary, who was pledged to be married to him and was expecting a child. 6While they were there, the time came for the baby to be born, 7and she gave birth to her firstborn, a son. She wrapped him in cloths and placed him in a manger, because there was no room for them in the inn.

8And there were shepherds living out in the fields nearby, keeping watch over their flocks at night. 9An angel of the Lord appeared to them, and the glory of the Lord shone around them, and they were terrified. 10But the angel said to them, "Do not be afraid. I bring you good news of great joy that will be for all the people. 11Today in the town of David a Savior has been born to you; he is Christ the Lord. 12This will be a sign to you: You will find a baby wrapped in cloths and lying in a manger."

13Suddenly a great company of the heavenly host appeared with the angel, praising God and saying, 14"Glory to God in the highest, and on earth peace to men on whom his favor rests."

15When the angels had left them and gone into heaven, the shepherds said to one another, "Let's go to Bethlehem and see this thing that has happened, which the Lord has told us about."

16So they hurried off and found Mary and Joseph, and the baby, who was lying in the manger. 17When they had seen him, they spread the word concerning what had been told them about this child, 18and all who heard it were amazed at what the shepherds said to them. 19But Mary treasured up all these things and pondered them in her heart. 20The shepherds returned, glorifying and praising God for all the things they had heard and seen, which were just as they had been told.

The Truth With No Words
Christmas 2010
Luke 2:1-20

As Liz Jackson wheeled her car into the parking lot, she felt a little surge of optimism. The place was practically empty. That wasn't too surprising, of course, since it was Christmas Eve and management was trying to get as many people out of the hospital for the holiday as possible – but it was, just maybe, a sign that she could get her work done in a timely fashion. That would be nice, since it was both Christmas Eve and payday. "If everything works out all right," she thought to herself, "I'll have both time and money to spare today. Nice!"

Liz worked with the hospital dieticians to make sure that each patient knew how to order the right food. Sometimes it was a challenge, as she had to explain more than once how to choose from among all the options on the "one-size-fits-all" menu that the hospital printed. Busy days meant long days. Fewer cars in the lot meant fewer visitors, and fewer visitors meant fewer people in the rooms, and fewer people in the rooms meant she could get in and out with no hassle. "Yep, it's going to be a good day at work," thought Liz.

She got up to the fourth floor west and headed towards room 469. As she drew near the doorway, however, she heard the sounds of a child's laughter mingled with someone singing *Wudolf the Wed-Nosed Wein-deer* in an Elmer Fudd voice. Liz knew that sometimes entertainers visited the children, and although it meant she'd have to stop back later, she was glad that her little friend had some company. Emily, the patient in 469, was the oldest child of a single mother who had just delivered twins. She spent a lot of time alone as she was recuperating from painful back surgery.

Not long after, Liz was just about to barge into room 480 when she overheard someone reading the Bible out loud. Although most of the preachers didn't seem to mind it when she had to interrupt their visits, Liz liked to give her patients the privacy of that time. She hadn't seen the minister come onto the floor, but someone was in there praying up a storm. She went back to the nurse's station to get caught up on some paperwork.

Liz was a little flustered when she tried to see the patient in room 476. Mrs. Weston was a widow in what Liz thought to be the end stages of cancer, and she knew that they had talked about calling in a team from hospice to help manage her pain. As she prepared to knock on the door, she overheard a man who sounded like a social worker talking to Mrs. Weston about what she might expect if she was moved to a residential hospice facility. "For a day with an empty parking lot," Liz thought, "there sure are a lot of people up on my floor!" Again, she didn't resent the patients getting visitors as much as she was surprised that the place was so full of guests when the lot seemed so empty.

Twenty minutes later, something clicked with her as she headed into room 472 and just about collided with a yellow housekeeping cart – and not just any yellow housekeeping cart, but one that had little coloring books and sudoku puzzles and word searches in a special folder. It occurred to Liz that every time that day she had tried to see a patient and had deferred to a visitor, that same cart had been in the hallway. And *that* meant that today, John was working on her floor.

So John, from housekeeping, was there. There was no entertainer, no pastor, no social worker. The fourth floor west was not overrun with an abundance of helpful visitors on Christmas Eve. It was just John, doing his thing. Liz paused for a moment to consider the fact that she didn't even know John's whole name – he was just "John, from housekeeping".

John was an interesting character. When people first saw him, to be honest, they were a little frightened. He had a big scar on his cheek, and you could see what looked to be some pretty impressive tattoos peeking out around the neckline of his shirt. But once he smiled, people knew that they had nothing to fear. John was quite simply the best human being that Liz (or most of the other people in the hospital) had ever met. It was John who was singing for the child in 469; it was John who had been praying with the family in 480; and it was John who had been trying to calm Mrs. Weston's fears about moving into hospice. He didn't always work four west, but when he did, it was a better day for everyone. John was one of those people who just knew everyone's names, from the patients to the doctors to the nurse's aides. And when John called you by name, and looked you in the eye, you had a sense that, for at least that part of the day, someone was paying attention. You *mattered*.

While Liz was glad to be sharing duty with John, it didn't really matter all that much to her that day. She was doing her best to get in and get out, and at the end of her shift, she was already ticking down the items on her shopping list when she saw it. As she walked towards her car in the lot, she noticed that the front left tire was completely flat. As she bent to examine it, she realized that she must have hit a pothole on the way in that morning, because the rim was bent. To make matters worse, she knew that she didn't have a spare – she'd taken that out of the trunk last week to make room for a few things she'd wanted to take over to her dad's.

Liz stood there and looked at her car, almost as if she could will the offending rim into shape. She didn't know what to do. She might still be there if John hadn't come circling down the ramp in his old Ford pickup. He saw the look on Liz's face and followed her eyes to the wheel. Without saying anything, he parked next to her and went to look for the spare.

"It's no use," Liz said. "I can't change the tire because I don't have a spare." She felt like an idiot.

John looked at the damaged wheel and said, "You know, this isn't that bad at all. There's a shop a couple of blocks up that will be open until five. Let's take it there." So John jacked up the car and took the misshapen wheel and threw it in the back of his truck. When they got to the repair shop, it was indeed open, and the owner seemed eager to do something for John. He told Liz that it'd be ready in forty-five minutes or so.

Liz started to thank John for his trouble as if she expected him to be leaving, but he looked at her and smiled and said, "Now hold on, Liz. I'm not going to let you try to get back to that garage and put this wheel on yourself. I think you're stuck with me for a while."

When Liz realized that was indeed the case, she said, "Well if that's what's happening, let's not sit here. Let's head over there –" she jerked her head in the direction of the donut shop across the street "- And get a cup of coffee or something."

Once they were settled into the booth, Liz screwed up her courage and went ahead and asked the question everyone on the floor had wanted to know for years. "John, why are you so…I mean, don't take this the wrong way or anything, but you are just, well, so *nice*. How did you get to be that way? Have you always been so…" she stuttered a bit, "so *good?*"

John let out a louder laugh than Liz had ever heard him offer before, and said, "Now what do you think, Liz? Do you think I've always been where I am now? Tell the truth!"

Liz allowed for the fact that he probably had not always been the angel of mercy and healing she had come to know. "So tell me, John. Where *does* it come from?"

John, who looked as if he could have been anywhere between forty-five and sixty-five years old, folded his hands on the table and told his story.

"When I was a young man, coming up," he said, "I was the one who pretty much ruled the roost in the neighborhood, if you know what I mean. I was a pretty good ballplayer, and in my neighborhood, that meant that I got whatever I needed. The better I got at ball, the more popular I was. Well, don't you know, I got too full of myself. Wound up getting kicked out of school, and then things just got worse. I did some time in juvie, and that really messed with my head. I was so focused on trying to be in the middle of everything, you know?"

"Anyway, my life headed downhill pretty fast. I was locked up as often as not for ten or fifteen years. But during my last incarceration, something clicked into place with me and I actually got some help. I signed up for a few courses, and when I was forty-three years old, I learned to read. Can you believe it? I had faked it for my whole life, but in a GED class in prison I learned to read."

"I got out of prison in November one year, and I was about as far from that cocky, confident kid I had been as could be. The first half of my life, I fought to be in the middle of the picture – the center of attention. I wanted to be in charge. But my time in lock-up, and the GED classes, and learning to read – that beat it into me. I felt like…no, I *knew* – that I was nothing special. I was insignificant. When I got out of prison, I was alone, friendless, and felt empty. And the first – and only – piece of mail I got that week was from my sponsor in the NA group I had to go to." As he said this, John pulled a laminated card out of his back pocket and unfolded it. He threw it on the table and invited Liz to examine it.

"It's not much," he said. "And I was never the type to care about old paintings. But something about the faces on that picture really got to me. Look at them. Okay, that's the baby Jesus and his mother, and here's this angel giving them a basket of wheat and grapes. And all three of them are looking at the basket. When I saw the title of the painting, *The Madonna of the Eucharist*, it struck me that the wheat and grapes stood for the bread and wine. The artist was trying to get a point across – that even though Jesus was just a baby, his body and his blood would be spilled."

"But I sat there looking at that picture for a while, and then I started to wonder. When the angel was giving Mary that basket, did Mary know what was ahead for Jesus? Did the angel? Or is it just a little snack? How much of the big picture did Mary see? I'm sure that Jesus, being only a baby, didn't get much of it at that point. Do you see what I mean?"

Liz smiled, aware of the improbability of having a discussion of Renaissance art with a hospital housekeeper while seated at the Donut World café on Christmas Eve.

"Who knew, and what did they know, when this picture was painted?" John asked. "Here's what I think: I think that nobody – not the angel, not Mary, not the baby – knew the full story of what was to come. But here's the deal: the painter knew. And because he knew, I knew. I could make a connection between the birth of Jesus and the death of the savior. I want to tell you, Liz, that painting is the best sermon I ever saw in my life."

Madonna of the Eucharist by Alessandro Botticelli, c. 1470

"So I saw that it was painted by a man named Botticelli, and I went to the library and Googled him. I wanted to learn a little more about him. And when I Googled him, I found this little poem."

John turned the tattered card over and there, laminated to the back, were a few lines of poetry:

i am a dot on
paper
a single simple
smallness
of one color
joining hands
with a million others
on the north edge of an
angel's eyelash
to show you a part of truth
with no words[1]

"That last part of the poem really got to me, Liz. The part about how sometimes truth has no words."

"You see, for most of my growing up, I thought that there was a picture, and that I was right in the middle of it. I was all that, if you know what I mean. And then I made all those mistakes, and I got stuck in prison and messed up on the drugs and, well, thirty years later I was pretty sure that there was no plan, no design, no picture at all."

"But somehow, seeing that painting reminded me that even though I can't see it all the time, I know that there *is* a big picture. And I know that somehow, somewhere, I'm *in* the big picture. Mostly, I don't see it. Mostly, I go to work and I go to my meetings and I go home, and I try to keep my nose clean and to be a blessing to someone during the day. But the reason that I can do that is because I trust that there is a big picture and someday, I'll get to see it. Just like one day, Mary learned all that there was to learn about Jesus. One day, that angel saw the truth about the one he had been called to serve. It all sounds so strange to me, but it feels so right to me, that I've decided that I needed to do my part – my little part – and tell the truth with no words.

Well, they got the tire fixed and Liz went shopping and got her errands done. That night, on Christmas Eve, she sat in church, and she

---

[1] Luci Shaw, "In A Botticelli Print" in *Listen To The Green* (Harold Shaw, 1971) p. 12.

thought about the events of her day. She thought about the painting, and about what John called "the big picture", and about truth with no words.

It occurred to her that so much of what qualifies as "the Christmas Spirit" these days is just noise. The Santa at the mall. The carols on the radio. The parties up and down her street as well as those at the hospital. Those things aren't bad, but they are just loud and bright.

But so much of what really matters about Christmas, it seemed to Liz, was the quiet parts. The congregation singing "Silent Night." *Silent Night.* Looking around the room at the candles. Watching a young mother hold her baby while they prayed for the child's father, a Marine who wouldn't be coming home this year.

Maybe the truest things, she thought, are quiet things. Maybe *she* could tell the truth without words.

After church, Liz was supposed to go over to her brother's house and join in the family gathering. And she did, eventually.

But first, she drove back to the hospital. And she went up to room 476, where Mrs. Weston lay flat on her back watching the plastic star as it glowed on her little Christmas tree. And Liz was somehow not very surprised to see John, from housekeeping, sitting there, with one tear on his scarred cheek. And for half an hour, it was a silent night. Nobody said anything – yet together, Liz and John told that frightened woman a part of the truth of Christmas. With no words.

A Stranger in My Manger
Luke 2:1-14
Christmas 1998

Dear Thaddeus,

Thank you for your last letter. I am glad to see that you are all right, especially in view of all the things that have happened in Jerusalem these past days. Please make sure that you keep yourself well, and stay out of trouble. You are my only son - I don't know what would happen to me if you were to get hurt . . . or worse.

In response to your question about the man named Jesus that some are calling the Messiah, yes, I have heard about him. I have known of this man for more than thirty years, to tell the truth. Perhaps it is time that you know the whole story.

It began years ago - just after your mother and I were married. You were not even born yet, and we had just settled into our home here in Bethlehem. The Romans had issued another of their ridiculous orders, this time for a census. Everyone had to go to their home town and register. It was a fiasco - no wonder Quirinius was sacked so quickly!

Well, here it was, the dead of winter, and all sorts of people are streaming into town. They had to have lodging, of course. And the enterprising people did what they could to make a profit - they rented out their rooms, their floor space, even their tents to travelers who needed a place to rest. This Jesus of whom you spoke was actually born in the little barn behind our house. It was quite a night - there were people coming and going all the time.

You might find it surprising that we should have had guests in that shed, normally reserved for our two oxen. The truth is, he didn't have to be born there. There were at least three other places that his parents had tried. I know, because I saw the whole thing.

The first place they went to was the house on the corner, you know, where the old woman Mariah used to live? She had three rooms and a barn - and no one was staying with her at all. I saw the tired man and his pregnant wife go to her door and knock. At first, she refused to answer. But they, like me, had seen the lamp glowing inside, and they knocked again. Finally, she answered. The man explained that he was here for the census, his wife was expecting their son, and could they please stay with her. She shook her head firmly, and said that she was too old to be bothered by the Romans and their census. She said that her home was hers and she wasn't about to let anyone in it, pregnant or not. She was sorry, she said, but she was too old to change. She just about slammed the door on the man before he had a chance to plead his case. Do you know, son, that I never saw anyone else enter that home until the day she died? It was like she closed it off forever that night.

Well, the man didn't have time to worry, he needed someplace to stay. So he went to the next home, where Isaac and Zilporah live. Their house was full, Isaac explained. He would have liked to help - I could see it in his eyes - but he said that there were already three families in their house. I heard the young woman - the pregnant one - ask if they could stay in the stable behind Isaac's home. When Zilporah heard this, she rushed out of the house and said that it was simply impossible. The stable was too dirty, too messy, she said. She said that it was a good idea, but she was too embarrassed to have anyone look into that part of their home. If the couple could come back the next day, she said, they would have the stable clean enough to be presentable; but as it stood, it was simply impossible for anyone to get into the barn then.

The man sighed, and gave his peace to Isaac and Zilporah. Then he trudged to the house next to ours. The old man Benjamin was there, and he, like Isaac, had already filled up his rooms. As he was closing the door to the couple, the man asked about HIS barn. Benjamin got a real thoughtful look on his face and said, "You know, I do have a barn. Let me go see what kind of shape it's in." At this, the young couple brightened a bit, and they agreed to wait at the door. Benjamin went through his house and out to the rear of his place. I saw him go into the barn, but then he never came out. After what seemed like at least thirty or forty minutes, I sneaked around to peer in through the doorway. Do you know what happened, Thaddeus? The old man had gone to check on the barn, but when he got there he must have discovered that his cow was sick or something. There he stood, massaging her udder, trying to soothe her. She was obviously in distress, and he was concerned. I didn't blame him . . . but the fact was, that he had gotten distracted. I went around to the front and the man was just standing there, looking like he was desperate. The woman was crying by this time. She was in great pain.

I'm not sure what made me do this, but I walked over to them and asked them if they needed a place to stay. Now, your uncle Moshe was here with his family, as were your grandparents and a cousin of mine. There was no room in our home. But I led the couple and their donkey to the shed out back and it was like I was showing them to a palace. It was a mess, of course. But the man must have known something about work, because while I was down the street getting some clean straw to keep them warm, he took it upon himself to get the place straightened up. It looked really, well, it looked almost nice by the time we were finished. We hung an old blanket over the doorway to give them some privacy and went to bed.

14

It wasn't too many hours after that when we heard the cries of the baby boy. Of course your mother was in the thick of things, helping to make sure that the child was warm and clean and that the young mother was doing all right. She must have sent me back and forth between the house and the shed a dozen times! On one of the trips, I met some shepherds who claimed that they had seen a vision of angels, and that this baby was to be the messiah. They went right into the shed and bowed in prayer with the parents -- with that baby propped up right there in the manger!! I didn't know what to think.

Well, after a few days, the man had completed his business and he and his wife and child left our town. I didn't think much about it until the next year, when that murderer Herod sent his troops into town and slaughtered all the baby boys - he must have heard the rumor about a messiah as well.

Last year, I went to Jerusalem to celebrate the Passover. It was a dream come true for me, as you know. On the way, I ran into this teacher they call Jesus. I saw his mother - they call her Mary - and I knew in a moment that it was the woman who had been in our shed so many years ago. I think that the shepherds were right. I think that he might be the one that will free us from the things that bind us.

Thaddeus, this is what I want you to do. I want to you learn from my experience of so many years ago. I want you to follow that man. Some of the people I know claimed that they were too busy to be bothered with him. Some were ashamed of the things that they had to offer to him, and so refused him. Some got distracted and simply forgot about him. Follow him, Thaddeus. Stay with him, and give him whatever you have. I do not know where it will lead you, but I am convinced that this is all Yahweh's doing. I cannot help but think that extending a greeting to that family so many years ago was perhaps the most important thing that I have ever done . . . and to think that like my neighbors, I might have missed that chance. My son, I do not want you to miss this. It is too important.

I know that some of what I have written may seem like a fairy tale. That's all right. If you are not too bitter, too busy, too ashamed, or too distracted to be with this man Jesus, I think you will see that he has much more to offer than bed-time stories. Follow him, Thaddeus. Follow him. And tell him I said, "hello."

Love and peace to you,

Father

I Am Alive
Luke 2:1-20
Christmas 1993

Ahhh, I see that I am not alone in my reflections this evening. This is a beautiful place, is it not? Oh, but if only you had seen it a year ago - if you had seen it when the sky was singing. I had hoped that someone would join me tonight - in part because I feel like talking, and in part because I've a message I need to send to Jericho.

What? You're on your way to Jericho? Please, please - would you take this with you? It's a letter - a letter to a little girl - or at least someone who was a little girl many years ago. Her name is Lydia, and she is the wife of the tanner. Let me explain.

I am a shepherd. My name is Amos. I was not always a shepherd, oh no. When I was nearly grown, my parents, who were merchants, both fell very ill. I was hustled off to live with my mother's cousin, a man who tended sheep and goats. Oh, how I hated that man, and how I hated that life. I couldn't wait to return. Then the word came that my parents had died. I had no place to go. I became a shepherd. I became what I hated.

One of the other men would sometimes bring his little girl up the hill to play her pipe for the sheep. She must have been about six or seven, I suppose. She sometimes spoke to me, I suppose because I was the closest to her in age. The last time she spoke to me, she said that she had had a dream about me. She said that she could not remember much, only that I was an old man and that I was singing.

Well, I must have reacted in a way that did not please her, because as I was laughing at the idea of myself being old and singing, she ran away. But listen, friend, and I will tell you. I had no intention of ever becoming old, and there had been no cause for singing in my life.

Not long after that night, I had to leave. I will not tell you why, but I will tell you that I am not proud of what happened. In fact, I am not proud of much that has happened in these past forty years. I will tell you this: I was alone, and I was afraid much of the time. But like many men who are alone and afraid, I did not act the part at all. No, I surrounded myself with loud people. I took foolish chances - it was almost as if I was determined to prove that little girl wrong. Her vision of me as an old man frightened me. There was no way that I could live, not feeling the way that I was feeling. And so I was always the first to try to fend off the lions as they came to steal the sheep - half-hoping that they would kill me, but deathly afraid that they would. I taunted and mocked the centurions as they passed,

17

but always ran or hid when they sought me out. I was always on the edge, always between life and death, always in fear. I neither had nor wanted faith.

And then, then -- well, let me read you the letter. You will see.

Dear Lydia:

Greetings to you, my little friend. I am Amos, the young shepherd of so many years ago. I hope you remember me. I surely remember you. And there is something I must tell you: I am an old man. I am not dead.

For years, my friend, this was the best and the worst that I could say about myself. How I hated the memory of that night when you shared your vision of me as an old man. How many times I have cursed you - blaming my failure to die on you.

And it is true, Lydia. I wanted to die. I went to sleep hoping that I would not wake up. But always something or someone dragged me into the next day.

And Lydia, I know now what - or who - had dragged me into all those tomorrows.

It was about a year ago that I found myself with a small band of shepherds on a hillside north of Bethlehem. We were passing the night as I have passed countless other nights when suddenly the skies became brighter than the brightest day. There was a presence, a man from God, who reached through my fear and pulled me into the light and told me that God had heard the cries of his people and had sent the Messiah. Lydia, all my life I would have told you that I had no need for a savior, but when the angel announced his arrival, I cried like a little baby - it was as if God himself had discovered my secret. Suddenly the messenger was joined by many others and the heavens were full of the most wonderful music. It was the most beautiful thing I had ever seen.

The angels told us how to find the baby, and we went to see this infant messiah. We met others there who had similar experiences. We spoke briefly, we watched, and then we went home.

I might have forgotten the impact of that night if I had not run into an old man named Simeon in the marketplace. He was some sort of prophet, and had just seen the baby at the temple. He, too, was convinced that the baby was the Messiah. As we talked, I began to like this old man. We have become friends - deep and fast friends in our old age. He has taught me a great deal. He has taught me how to read, and has shown me in the scriptures God's promise of a savior. He has taught me how to pray - and Lydia, I know that my prayers are heard. And this is important - because in his teaching me the scriptures and in his teaching me to pray, this old man has taught me how to believe. He has taught me how to trust in a God who loves me and who calls to me. He has taught me to have faith in places where I cannot see with my eyes. He has taught me to sing in my heart when my words cannot contain the meaning. He has taught me to hope for the day when God's messiah will reign in men's hearts everywhere. He has taught me how to live!

Now, Lydia, my heart beats differently. I am no longer dragged into tomorrow. I have seen the messiah. I have sung with the angels.

Yes, Lydia, you were right. I am an old man. I am not dead. But more than that, my friend, I am alive. I am alive!

Well, I have rested on this hillside long enough, my friends, and I must move on. Thank you for listening to an old man. And thank you for taking this to Lydia. Wait here a bit longer. And keep praying, my friends. Keep hoping. It may be that God will bless you with a vision of his messiah this season. It may be that you will sing with the angels. Rest assured that the savior has come - and he is looking for you. Peace to you this night.

Freed
Christmas 2007
Luke 2:1-14

When the commercial for the latest Will Smith movie was over, Isaiah Weary put down the television remote and reached for the old black leather journal that was never far away. He turned to a page near the middle of the old book and carefully added the name to his list: I. M. Legend.

Ever since he'd been 'hooked on phonics' as a child he liked to imagine names and identities for himself. After all, when your parents name you Isaiah Michael, they are sort of setting you up. Your initials are I. M. "I am what?" you ask yourself.

And when your name is a word that sounds like one word – "wary" – and is spelled like another word – "weary" – you start to think, "well, am I? Am I wary? Am I weary?"

For most of his life, Isaiah Michael Weary had collected alternative identities as he went through the various tasks of his day. When he met a word, or saw a name, he wondered if maybe that was who he was, or at least who he could be. He started by scrawling the words on the margins of his notebooks in school – daydreaming, really. If someone were to have peeked at his sixth grade papers, for instance, they'd see scribbles like "I. M. Awesome!" or "I. M. Lost". In the more private places of his little book, there were other words: "Lonely", "Nervous", "Frayed" are but a few examples.

Now, to be fair to Isaiah, it's not like he obsessed about this as an adult. But every now and then, when he saw a new one, he jotted it down in his book. He didn't know why, really. Maybe he secretly was looking for a new identity.

I. M. Legend. He liked the sound of that one. He hadn't seen the movie, of course, but the actor looked brave, and tough, and sufficient. He wished for that to be true of himself.

Most of his life, he'd done pretty well living into the identity that he felt his parents had given to him. Isaiah Michael Weary *was* wary. All his life, he had been concerned that he was somehow screwing things up, or making a mistake, or that somehow things would get ruined in the end.

In high school, for instance, he was probably the most talented trumpet player in the band, but nobody knew, because he didn't play loudly enough to be heard except when he was alone. In college, he had been in love with an amazing woman, but she never knew anything about it, because he couldn't speak that relationship into being. He didn't want to risk being hurt.

In every aspect of his life, it seemed, he was playing it conservative. He never let the gas tank get below a quarter full, he always rounded up when he was tipping so that no one thought he was cheap, his insurance policy had the maximum payout and the lowest deductible…all of these were symptoms of the dis-ease he so often felt. Something terrible was going to happen. He was almost always nervous, And because Isaiah Michael Weary was so wary, he was also often weary. Very weary.

That's why he was at home on this particular December 23rd, in fact. He had been invited to a neighbor's Christmas party. Mark was a nice enough guy – he and his wife lived at the end of the hallway in their apartment building – but Isaiah couldn't believe that he was really wanted at the gathering. Mark had mentioned it to him in the hallway after inviting the Johnsons across the hall, and Isaiah thought that he was merely being polite. He didn't want to intrude, and he didn't want to be rejected, so he was at home, channel surfing. After the movie commercial ended, he hit upon a real classic: one of the cable networks was doing a marathon of the Charlie Brown Christmas special. Isaiah had come upon it right as Charlie Brown screamed out, "Isn't there anyone who knows what Christmas is all about?" And Linus van Pelt responds by reciting the Christmas story from Luke's gospel – the part about the angels and the shepherds and the baby.

Now Isaiah had never been a particularly religious person – he just couldn't bring himself to believe in much of anything, to be honest. But as he watched this ancient cartoon, he was struck by a part of the story that was simply impossible for him to believe: "and the angel of the Lord said unto them, 'Fear not…'"

Isaiah Michael Weary knew better. To live is to fear. To exist is to worry. "Fear not?" Yeah, right! I. M. Weary did not want this sort of existential challenge from a cartoon, and so he popped the button on the remote and the set fell silent. And for a few moments, Isaiah was so distracted that he began to think about all of the things that he was, in fact, afraid of: He was afraid that his 401(k) plan was losing value; he sensed that the landlord would be increasing the rent; he was scared to death that the war would expand; he was worried that one of the leading Republican candidates was going to be the next President. He was also worried that one of the leading Democratic candidates was going to be the next President. He worried about an economic slump that would cost him his job. He wondered what he would do if he were fired.

And so it happened that, lost in thought, I. M. Weary was surprised by Mark's head popping through the door. "Hey, neighbor, are you coming to the party tonight?"

Isaiah panicked. "Uh, well, no. I can't – tomorrow is Christmas Eve, and, well, I'm just not ready. In fact, I'm on my way out now. Yep, I'd say I'm booked solid for the next 24 hours or so…"

Mark looked genuinely disappointed. "Oh, that's too bad…" and then his face brightened. "Say, if you're booked for the next 24 hours, does that mean that in about 27 hours you'd be free to come to the midnight candlelight service at church with us?"

Oooooh. Isaiah was afraid. He didn't really want to go, but he didn't want to say "no", either. He didn't want to look like a jerk when it was becoming at least somewhat plain that Mark was willing to spend time with him. So, feeling like there were no other options, Isaiah said, "Um…yes?"

And that's how it came to be that at about 11:34 the following evening, Christmas Eve, Isaiah Michael Weary found himself sitting in the rigid pews of the local Methodist church listening to the pastor read the exact same passage from Luke's gospel that he had heard the night before. He must have been exceptionally fidgety or irked, because it was apparent to Mark, who asked him in the car on the way home, "Is everything all right? Is anything bothering you?"

And something remarkable happened early on Christmas morning that year. Isaiah Michael Weary – perhaps because he was, in fact, so weary, told the truth. He simply said, "Mark, I don't want to be rude, but you know, I just can't buy all that religion stuff. It's not for me. And tonight, especially, the whole 'Fear not from the angels on high' bit. How can that be? I don't have a recession-proof job. I watch the news. That's nonsense. My whole life I'm running scared, and here's some heavenly cherub in pajamas and wings telling people to 'Fear not.' I'm just not interested in that."

Mark laughed and said, "You know, Isaiah, that's the best part of the story so far as I'm concerned. For a long time, I, too was running scared. But somehow, the Lord broke into my life and I learned a new way of living – a way that was not defined by the things that I was worried about."

Isaiah was petrified now. He was interested in Mark's story, but he sure didn't want to be preached to. He wasn't looking for any kind of conversion. Mostly, he just wanted the night to be over. Isaiah shook his head warily, and said, "Well, you can talk about it like it's not much, but I just don't think I'll ever get that."

But Mark wasn't pressing, and he wasn't shying away, either. "It's not all at once, you know," he said. "Even Jesus said that life in God's presence is like being 'born again'. I take that to mean that it's starting with baby steps and little things. For me, it was just agreeing to show up in worship once a week and getting together with a group of friends who wanted to live life the same way that I did – God's way. And we've agreed to tell each other the truth."

Isaiah hedged. "I don't know," he said. "That sounds like a pretty big commitment – a pretty big risk to me." And while his heart pounded within him, Isaiah was torn between wishing that this conversation would end immediately and being afraid that it might do just that. He blurted out, "So that's it – you just change? You just say, 'OK, God, I believe', and everything is just ok? That sounds like a load of –"

"No, no – that's not it. Listen, Isaiah, if you are content with your life as it is, then great. I'm happy for you. But I sense that maybe you're not perfectly happy. I asking you to take one small step into something new. What if you started with me? What if you came to church on Sunday as my friend. Start with one Sunday, one friend. Just one step."

Isaiah wanted, for the first time in his life, to say "yes". But he couldn't – not right away. So he said, "Look, why does this matter to you? I'm just a guy who lives in your apartment building. I'm nothing."

And Mark smiled and said, "You know, we Isaiah's have to stick together."

"What are you talking about? Your name is Mark!"

"People call me Mark because I'm a 'Junior'. My dad is Isaiah M., and I'm I. Mark. My full name is Isaiah Mark Freed."

That hit Isaiah like a ton of bricks. Slowly, he said, "So your first two initials are the same as mine?"

Mark knew exactly what Isaiah was referring to, and smiled. "That's right. I. M. Freed. Pretty cool, huh?"

I. M. Freed. The name hung in the air, and echoed in his mind. In his head, Isaiah walked around it as if it were a three-dimensional piece of art that had been mounted just for him. It was a name that had never occurred to him before. But it was one that he liked. One that he wanted.

And then he found himself at home. And as Isaiah thought about the events of the past two days, he reached again for the little black journal. He wrote one final new name on its pages, slowly and clearly: I. M. Freed.

Shepherd's Local Number 2:20
Luke 2:1-20
Christmas 2003

The young man set down his can of Pepsi and looked across the table at the face of the older woman. He felt like he ought to be angry, but instead, all he felt was relief and maybe even gratitude. She repeated her question.

"So then, Eric, do we understand each other? You know what's expected here?"

"Yes, Aunt Florence, I do. And I want you to know, I really will try my best to make it work here." He was a bit embarrassed about having to come and live with his aunt. Yet with all the community service hours he needed to complete in order to avoid serving time in jail, it made sense to stay with her here in the city. He just couldn't believe that she was being so cool about it. After all, her brother, Eric's father, had flipped.

Florence looked at the newspaper she'd been holding idly. Eric glanced around the room, wondering exactly what he was supposed to be doing at that very moment. He was sure he didn't want to do the wrong thing, though.

He glanced at his aunt again, and something on her lapel caught his eye. It was a tiny pin with the numbers 2 2 0 etched on to it. He remembered seeing it some years before - evidently, she wore it often.

"Aunt Florence, what's up with that pin? Is your birthday or anniversary or something on February 20th?"

Florence, who looked to be in her forties, laughed. "No, that's not it. Let me tell you about this pin, Eric. Maybe it will help you feel better about what you've got to do."

"I got it about twenty years ago. I had been working as a Nurse's Aide at an old folks home over on Route 219. It was a horrible place to

27

work, at least at first. That summer it was so hot, and most of the rooms didn't have any air conditioning. I can't imagine how it would have been to live there."

"I didn't really want to work at the home. To me, it was just another in a series of lousy jobs I'd been having. Your uncle and I hadn't met yet, and to be honest, it was not a good time in my life. I was drinking quite a bit and, well, let's just say that not all of my choices were good ones."

Eric, whose ears had perked up a bit at the thought of his aunt being a party animal, couldn't help but grin. Florence went on.

"I had been a nurse's aide in a couple of those homes. It was terrible. The wages were low, and it seemed like you couldn't get anything right. If it wasn't the patients complaining about the way you changed their sheets or the bedpan, it was their families griping about how they paid so much money to care for grandpa and he doesn't deserve this... And in most of the places I'd been, you also had the staff barking out orders. The 'real' nurses often had a real attitude, the place smelled like a morgue...Most of the time, it was just terrible. So I'd work in one home for a while, then get fired and catch on with another. It's not like those places are overwhelmed with people to do their work, you know."

"But this place wasn't like that. Oh, don't get me wrong. Patients and their families still complained. It smelled bad. And the money was lousy. But there was just a sense that somehow, things were different. The spirit was better. The staff seemed to get along. It was the first time in my life where I felt like the people I worked with really cared about me. And it wasn't just me. One girl was going through a rough time at home and someone else let her move in for a few weeks. Another girl lost her baby and couldn't work for a couple weeks, and the other people just took her shifts so she wouldn't lose her job. There seemed to be six or seven women who really helped the place have a different kind of feel."

"So I said to one of these women, 'Look, I've worked in a couple of places, but this one's different. What's up with that?' And she just got a stupid little grin on her face and said, 'Well, I don't know, unless it's the union.' And then she went to check on a patient."

"I'd been there a few months, and I knew for a fact that they hadn't been taking any money out of my pay for union dues. And I knew that there was no real difference in my salary from any other home I'd worked in. If there were no dues and no benefits, was there really a union?"

"So the next day I saw her with a couple of her friends, and I said, 'Listen, Ellen. What's this about a union? I never heard nothing about a union here.' Her friends all looked at me, and then at her. And then I noticed that they all had these little pins with a 2:20 on them. I said, 'Why haven't I heard anything about this union? Can I join?' And Ellen says to me, 'Look, Flo, if you want to know about the union, come with me tomorrow night. I'll talk to you about it then.'"

"'Tomorrow night?' I said. 'That's Christmas Eve! What kind of a union has a meeting on Christmas Eve?' One of the other girls smiled and said, 'That's the only time that the Shepherd's Local Number 2:20 ever meets!' And then they all laughed and walked away."

"Well, what could I do? I had to find out. So Ellen agreed to pick me up for dinner and the meeting. She came, and after we had a bite of dinner, she led me straight to a church! When I realized we were heading for the sanctuary, and not the basement I was embarrassed and a little angry, but she just marched me down and sat beside me. When the kid was reading in the bible, she nudged me right when he got to verse 20 in Luke chapter two. 'That's us,' she said. 'The shepherds.' As if I was supposed to understand what *that* was about."

"So then the preacher gets going, and it turns out he's talking about shepherds, too. Now Eric, I don't know about you, but I can't tell a sheep from a goat from a cow. I never been on a farm and don't need to go. But he started talking about these shepherds that went to see the baby Jesus, and he said that in that day, the Shepherds had a bad reputation. They spent all their time outside the village guarding other people's property. But because they were outside the village, they couldn't maintain all of the spiritual laws of the time, and so the religious people thought that they were unclean. The preacher said that most people agreed that shepherds were such liars that no shepherd was ever allowed to testify in court."

"It seemed to me that these guys really got a raw deal. I mean, here they were taking care of other people's most valuable possessions, but the owners of the sheep thought they were too good for the shepherds. The shepherds were the ones freezing out there night after night, but nobody would give them the time of day."

"And as that preacher went on, it occurred to me that maybe me and the girls at work, we were like shepherds too. I mean, here we were, caring for grandma or grandpa. Everybody said that they loved these old people, but nobody wanted to be around to change a messy bed or help wipe someone else's bum. They paid us poorly and treated us like dirt -

heck, most of them never even said thank you. Just like the shepherds, we were sort of the 'underclass'. The low-lifes."

"So the next day, of course, was Christmas. And like most Christmases, I was at work. I sat down with Ellen at lunch and I said, 'I get it! 2:20 Shepherds - it's an inside joke, right? We're the shepherds, aren't we?'"

"'It's no joke,' she said. 'You're right, we're in the story, but let me tell you two things about that story. First, do you remember what happened when Jesus was born?'"

"'Hey, Ellen, I know I'm not super religious, but give me a little credit, OK? There was all kinds of singing and bright lights and angels and stuff, right?'"

"And Ellen said, 'Well, sort of. That's what the shepherds saw. But what about Mary and Joseph? Weren't they just another poor, homeless couple? Weren't they just alone in the barn worrying about the baby? From what the Bible says, they didn't know anything about any lights, any singing, or any angels.'"

"I interrupted her: 'But the shepherds told them, didn't they!'"

"'They did', she said. "Think about that for just a moment. Of all the people in all the times and all the places of the world, God chose not only to use these shepherds - these men who were really on the fringe of the life in the world at that time - to witness God's glory, but to share that great news with the rest of the world. It makes me laugh, a little. The shepherds, who couldn't even testify in court, were supposed to tell Mary and Joseph what they had seen. But when they went to the stable, they told the truth, and that confirmed to Mary and Joseph what they had been told much earlier. Do you see?'"

"'Yeah, I get it. That's one thing. What's the other thing?'"

"Ellen asked me, 'What did you and I do after worship last night?' And I said, 'You know as well as I did that church didn't get over until after midnight and we started here at 6:30 this morning. We came to work, that's what we did!'"

"And Ellen pulls out this little Bible from her purse and says, 'And that's the same thing that the shepherds did. Look at what it says in Luke 2:20: *And the shepherds returned, glorifying and praising God for all they had heard and seen, as it had been told to them.*'"

"'Look, Flo, you asked about the union. There isn't any, at least none like you're thinking of, anyway. But there are a group of us who believe the truth in the story that you heard at church last night - that God loved the world enough to send his Son to die, that we might live. And we've got a name for ourselves, the Shepherd's Local Number 2:20."

"So you're not really a Union...' I interrupted."

"'Oh, but we are. We do what the shepherds did, is all. We come to work and we do our best to glorify God in our work. You know the people that we see - the patients and their families? They're like Mary and Joseph to us. They can't see the angels, so much. They can't hear the singing. But they need to know the Good News. So that's what I do. I share the Good News in the things that I say and the things that I do.'"

"And Eric, Ellen and I talked a long time that day and the day after. And I told her that I wanted to become a Christian - that the God who trusted shepherds would probably put up with someone like me. And she prayed with me. And the next day, she gave me this little pin and said, 'Welcome to the Shepherd's Local Number 2:20, Flo!"

"And you ask your Dad, Eric, but that's when my life was changed. I left the nursing home a long time ago, when your cousins were born. But I never forgot that Christmas story. Ever since then, I've thought of myself as a shepherd. You know, I'm not the most polished person in the family. I'm certainly not the richest. But I know what I've seen and heard. And I'll share it with others. And any time someone needs a place to stay - like you, for instance - well, my door is open."

Every now and then over the next couple of days, Eric had some question or other about the Bible for his aunt. Then, on Wednesday, he asked if he could go with her to the Christmas Eve service at the church. When he went to get in the car, there was a little box on the front seat. He opened it up to find a little button with the numbers 2-2-0 etched onto it. And he put it on.

So far as I know, the nursing home on route 219 has closed down. But Shepherd's Local Number 220 is still accepting members. If you'd like to join, all you've got to do is look for where God is moving in the world. Listen to the places where God might be singing, or look for the lights God might be shining. And do your best to show that to others. And live, trusting in his willingness to use imperfect people like you and me.

I've Got to Tell Somebody!
Luke 2:1-20
Christmas 1994

Don't tell anybody . . . that makes me laugh! It sounds like my mother.

"Now Simon - you must never speak of this again! You cannot tell anyone what we have done. You must keep the secret!"

That's what she said to me that night so long ago-more than thirty years ago, in fact. And now -- to think that I am here in jail - this cold, dark jail - because of the secret that's not so secret anymore. Of course I must laugh! What else can I do but laugh?

I should tell you my story. Perhaps you will find it interesting. Perhaps not - but we are in jail . . . so you can't run away from me!

My name, as I have said, is Simon. I live not far from here, in Bethlehem. My father is an innkeeper, and has been for many years. In fact, his is the inn that is mentioned in the story that Luke tells. In fact, his story is where my own story starts.

We were new in Bethlehem. Father had been a fisherman in Joppa until he was stricken with a disease that withered his hand. Mending nets is hard enough -- but with only one hand it was impossible. So we came to Bethlehem for a fresh start. Father, along with my mother, myself, and the baby would work the inn together. Those were hard days - we were so poor. I think that's why mother was so afraid that night - the night the pregnant woman and her fiancé came in.

We were just getting some business in the community. It was hard for a newcomer - a lame one at that - to establish respect. But we were getting by. Father and mother were so afraid that if they let that young couple stay in our home then we would be disgraced - the council would see to that. And then we'd have to start all over again.

But mother couldn't turn them away, either. She and my father led them quietly to the stable out behind the inn. It was plenty warm in there, and even though I was only six years old, I had spread fresh straw in the manger earlier that day. Mother gave them some blankets and some food and explained that there was simply no room - no room for them -- in our house.

Then we came inside and she told me -- my word, how she told me -- that I was not to go outside again that evening. "You must keep the secret", she said. "You must never tell what has happened here - we will be ridiculed." And she sent me up to bed.

I woke up a few hours later - at first I thought that it was Father's snoring that had wakened me, but as I listened I heard what sounded like crying -- a baby's cry. Yes, I was sure of it. It was so close. I crawled to the window and looked out, and for a moment I forgot about the noise because I saw the brightest star I have ever seen in my life. It seemed to hang only inches from my face. I have never seen such brilliance. It was beautiful. I heard the cry again, and realized that it was coming from our stable.

Then I saw a group of shepherds wandering around outside - that bothered me. Those shepherds are a pretty rough group, and many of them are looking for trouble. Sometimes they'd get drunk and try to sleep it off in somebody's barn -- sleep it off after a few fights, that is. They seemed to be heading right for the stable! Mother and Father were asleep - but I didn't want those thugs to hurt that new baby. I sneaked through the window and went straight for the stable. I thought that maybe I could warn the man, anyway.

By the time I got to the doorway of the stable and peeked around the corner, the baby had stopped crying. They were in there all right. But they weren't drunk. At first I thought they were talking to the man, but then I saw that they were simply looking at the baby. Nobody said anything. In the soft light of that brilliant star, I saw these shepherds kneel down and pray. After a few moments, they got up and came straight at me. They were clearly happy -- smiling, laughing, and one of them was even singing a psalm! I ducked into the shadows and watched them leave.

After they left, I took one more peek into the stable. I could see the small family now. The mother - a girl of about fifteen or so - was the most beautiful person I have ever seen. She wasn't pretty, nor handsome. She wasn't even all that attractive. But her eyes - and in that light - she was simply beautiful.

The man, the woman, and the baby all appeared to be ready for bed. They lay down, and it seemed as if there would be nothing further to interest a six-year old that night. Besides, my feet were getting cold on the stone walkway.

The next day they left, and I kept my promise to mother -- I didn't tell anyone about that night. I had almost forgotten it - after all, it didn't seem too important.

34

Yesterday, though, I remembered it all. I was on my way into the synagogue when I saw a huge man surrounded by a large crowd. He was speaking to them quite earnestly about something. Suddenly he took hold of a boy who was on crutches, laid his hands on him, and the boy was made well! Several people were healed before my very eyes. I drew closer and learned that this man was named Peter, and that he was a follower of Jesus, whom he called the Christ. He used the scriptures to explain that God had sent his own son into the world to make us friends with God again -- to show us love and peace in a way that the old sacrifices never could.

I listened to Peter all day, and came to believe that God does love me and would forgive me of all my sin. I prayed with Peter, and I felt all new and clean - I felt fresh in my faith. I was so happy that when Peter left the synagogue I followed him. He led me to a meeting room with about two hundred other people in it and we shared a meal - a simple meal of bread and wine. They all said so much about the things that this man - this son of God named Jesus- had done, and how he was the way that God had used to restore the world to himself.

Finally, I rose to leave. As I got to the door, I noticed a woman of about forty or fifty. She was a plain woman, but something about her made me take special notice -- and then she looked at me and I saw those eyes. I knew that I had seen them somewhere before. I realized that she was the one whom I had seen all those years ago -- hers was the baby that I had seen! When I got closer to her, I heard someone mention that she was the mother of this Jesus.

I could not believe it! It all came back - the brightness of the star, the prayers and joy of the shepherds, and the look of peace on her face. The savior of the world -- God's messiah -- the son of God--- he had been born in my backyard! I had seen him! I had been there!

Early today I went back to the synagogue with Peter. I had to learn more about this Jesus. Oh, how I longed to tell the news of God's love to everyone I saw! Many people came to our group today, and the disciples of Jesus healed them and spoke to them about forgiveness. Suddenly, though, the temple police came up to us and arrested us all. They've tossed us here in jail - the leaders of the synagogue are so angry. They must be jealous or afraid of Peter and the others - but they have forbidden us to speak of the name of Jesus ever again!

"Don't tell anybody!" they said. "Ha!"

"You must never talk to anyone about that name again." Like I said, it reminds me of my mother's warnings and her fears so many years ago.

Don't tell anyone! How can that be? How can I know of God's love and keep it to myself? How can anyone stay in the dark when he's seen the light?

I kept that promise to mother so many years ago - I didn't tell people what I had seen - until tonight. But now I must tell someone - I must, or I'll simply die of excitement. I must share the joy that God has given me.

But listen - I have been talking long enough. I will close. I will give you peace, now. Even we prisoners need peace, right?

But it is so dark in here. Can we share the light? Will you open your heart to this one called Jesus tonight? Will you accept the light of his star and pass it on to others? If you will, we can perhaps defeat the darkness and the cold of this place.

See, I have a candle. Jesus said, "I am the light of the world." Please, will you join me? Will you share the light?

When we join together with our candles – each with one tiny flame – we see how the power of darkness is really no power at all. Even the smallest candle can defeat it. How wonderful! Oh, it reminds me of the brightness of that star so many years ago.

I suppose that both mother and the Temple Police and synagogue leaders are angry now…because I have told. But what else could I do? If they keep me here the rest of my life, I will tell, because I know the power of the Light. No prison can be dark if we hold that Light in our hearts. Thanks be to God!

Reflection: The Fear of the Lord

There's a phrase in Hebrew: **Yir-aw YHWH**. It is usually translated as "The fear of the Lord." We find it nearly 140 times in Old Testament alone. When we speak of the "fear of the Lord", we don't understand that to be fear as terror, but rather fear as a sense of awe and wonder. It may be that kind of fear that the shepherds felt when, as Luke tells us,

And, lo, the angel of the Lord came upon them, and the glory of the Lord shone round about them: and they were sore afraid. (Luke 2:9, KJV)

It's a complicated term, and it's not really sensible in English. You've felt it. It happens when there is an encounter with the Holy – like when you're holding a baby for the first time, and you are speechless. You are living a prayer. You either want to shut up and bask in it or you want to scream because it's so beautiful. Either way, it's the same thing – **Yir-aw-YHWH**.

I feel it at every year at the Christmas Eve candlelight worship...I know it won't last. I know it can't last. Maybe on Christmas Eve I'm even a little worried about what's going to happen in the next 12 or 24 hours. But for a moment each year, I want to linger.

I'm not much for New Years Resolutions, but in the year to come, I want to learn more about **Yir-aw YHWH**. I want to live in that kind of wonder, because I am coming to see that **Yir-aw YHWH** is the only antidote to the kinds of fear that the world is selling me every day. You and I both know that "the fear of the Lord" is not the only fear that we encounter each day...that our culture, our political system, our economic climate, our environment...that everyone has some vested interest in making us afraid: afraid that we're going to be broke; afraid that we're ugly or fat; afraid that we're going to burn up; afraid that the wrong guy will get elected to office; afraid that your car is not shiny enough to attract the pretty girls; afraid that the other kids are all laughing at you behind your back.

But if we have the fear of the Lord, maybe all those other fears can be held in check. I'm pretty sure that there are no "how-to" books here. It seems to me that it's a life-style. A pathway. So this Christmas, I'll be taking a step – one step, at least, from fear as terror to fear as freedom. My hope is that in the year to come, I'll be able to see something each day with a sense of awe and wonder and reverence. And in that awe, I hope to know more about grace and peace – the gifts of Christmas.

Matthew 2:1-18

1After Jesus was born in Bethlehem in Judea, during the time of King Herod, Magi from the east came to Jerusalem 2and asked, "Where is the one who has been born king of the Jews? We saw his star in the east and have come to worship him."

3When King Herod heard this he was disturbed, and all Jerusalem with him. 4When he had called together all the people's chief priests and teachers of the law, he asked them where the Christ was to be born. 5"In Bethlehem in Judea," they replied, "for this is what the prophet has written: 6" 'But you, Bethlehem, in the land of Judah, are by no means least among the rulers of Judah; for out of you will come a ruler who will be the shepherd of my people Israel.'"

7Then Herod called the Magi secretly and found out from them the exact time the star had appeared. 8He sent them to Bethlehem and said, "Go and make a careful search for the child. As soon as you find him, report to me, so that I too may go and worship him."

9After they had heard the king, they went on their way, and the star they had seen in the east went ahead of them until it stopped over the place where the child was. 10When they saw the star, they were overjoyed. 11On coming to the house, they saw the child with his mother Mary, and they bowed down and worshiped him. Then they opened their treasures and presented him with gifts of gold and of incense and of myrrh. 12And having been warned in a dream not to go back to Herod, they returned to their country by another route.

13 When they had gone, an angel of the Lord appeared to Joseph in a dream. "Get up," he said, "take the child and his mother and escape to Egypt. Stay there until I tell you, for Herod is going to search for the child to kill him."

14 So he got up, took the child and his mother during the night and left for Egypt, 15 where he stayed until the death of Herod. And so was fulfilled what the Lord had said through the prophet: "Out of Egypt I called my son."

16 When Herod realized that he had been outwitted by the Magi, he was furious, and he gave orders to kill all the boys in Bethlehem and its vicinity who were two years old and under, in accordance with the time he had learned from the Magi. 17 Then what was said through the prophet Jeremiah was fulfilled:

18 "A voice is heard in Ramah, weeping and great mourning,
   Rachel weeping for her children and refusing to be comforted,
     because they are no more."

Dangerous Love[2]
Isaiah 9:2-7, Matthew 2:1-12
Christmas 2005

"Don't get me wrong, Dave," the professor told me. "I'm perfectly open to the claims of Jesus. I might even consider becoming a Christian myself…but the thing is, I don't know if I've ever met one."

We were sitting in the corner of a mostly-empty coffee shop and the wind was howling outside. I had thought that it was warmer inside the cozy room, but this woman's comment had caught me off-guard. What could she mean, she'd never met a Christian? What was I, chopped liver? Hello?!?! I'm right here! I'm a Christian.

I don't know what my face looked like, but I tried to play it cool. "Look, Claire," I said. "I know that there are some black marks in the church's past, but don't get overly dramatic here. Surely you're not saying that you've never seen anyone follow Jesus…"

This would have been the perfect opportunity for her to say, "Well, of course I'm not saying that, Dave! Why, after all, you're a Christian, and you follow Jesus impeccably…" Except that's not what she said. What she said was, "Look, Dave, I'm not trying to ruin your Thanksgiving or anything, but the truth is that the church just isn't a safe place." She went on to share with me a very painful story about how her family had been bruised by a group of people in the church who were so sure that they were right that they didn't seem to care much for those on the outside. She concluded by saying, "The church is awfully good at letting the world know what you're *against*. What is it, exactly, that you're *for*?"

I knew the situation she'd endured. She was right – the church had grievously wounded her family. I took a deep swallow of coffee and asked myself, "How did this happen? How did we in the church get to be the haters? Why is it that people are so afraid?"

Before I could respond, a man who'd been sitting in a nearby overstuffed chair shuffled to our table and sat down. "*Pardonnez-moi*," he said. "Forgive me for intruding. I do not know you, but I must confess that I've been eavesdropping – he smiled. May I share a story with you?"

---

2 The events in this story relating to the town of Le Chambon are all true. Primary source material for this story is Phillip Hallie's *Lest Innocent Blood Be Shed* (Harper Torchbooks 1979).

We invited the man to sit down, asked Sue to refill our coffee cups, and he began.

"You know about World War II," he said. "You have heard the stories of how the German army rounded up millions of people – Jews, Gypsies, homosexuals – and herded them into concentration camps. You know that millions of people died in the event we call the Holocaust...

"*Je suis un Chambonnais!* I am from Le Chambon – it is a tiny village, isolated in the mountains of southeastern France. Le Chambon was called 'the safest place for Jews in all of Europe.' Have you heard of Le Chambon?"

Neither Claire nor I had heard of this town, and as she warmed her hands on her coffee mug, I prompted the Frenchman to continue.

"It all began on a cold morning in the winter of 1940-41," he leaned forward, but his gaze was distant. "There was a knock at the door of the village parsonage, and the pastor's wife opened the door to find a desperate-looking woman, coated with snow and hollow with hunger. She brought the poor creature inside and learned that she was a German Jew who had come hundreds of miles, fleeing the death she sensed was certain inside Hitler's Germany. She asked the Pastor's wife for help.

"The Pastor's wife – her name was Magda – was a no-nonsense woman. She left the foreigner by the fire and went straight to the Mayor's Office, where she expected that the Mayor would help her plan for the refugee's future. The Mayor, however, had other thoughts – and said to Magda, 'How dare you endanger the welfare of the entire village for one foreigner! You must expel her at once!'

"Magda, of course, did no such thing. Instead, she went home and discussed the situation with her husband, the Rev. André Trocmé. Since the Mayor knew that the Jewish woman was in town, and since he thought that her presence was illegal, the only thing they could do was to get her out of town quickly. Using a network of friends in other villages, they gave the woman a few *francs* and some bread and sent her to the next village.

"But before long, there was another foreign woman. And then more. And before too long, the one o'clock train was full of Jews from all over Europe who had heard that there were people in Le Chambon who would help. Pastor André developed a network of thirteen Bible studies that were led by the young men of the parish. He met with these young men frequently...and steered the refugees to them. The young people, in turn, hid the Jewish visitors in homes and barns throughout the village and helped them make arrangements for the trek across the mountains to the freedom and safety of Switzerland. Whenever he got wind of a police sweep through the region, the Pastor would call for a meeting of his Bible Study leaders. The young men would race through the village alerting the townspeople, who then either secreted their guests in attics or sent them hiding in the dense forest outside of town.

"The entire village – even, eventually, a few of the policemen – became united under the Pastor's preaching. He just kept saying that the basic truth had been revealed in the life of Jesus Christ: that each human is important in the eyes of God – important enough, in fact, for God to send his only son to die for. And if a man was worth the love of Jesus, Pastor said, that man was surely worth our love and care.

"The Germans knew, of course, what was happening. They knew because the Pastor told them: 'We are helping the Jews to find freedom and safety. We think you should stop harming them.' And that so angered the Germans! They sent patrols into town, but never found any Jews!

"One day the leader of the Reformed Church in France came to visit Le Chambon, and sat with Pastor Trocmé. He said very bluntly, 'You are to stop helping the refugees.'

"Trocmé replied, 'You don't understand! These people – particularly the Jews – are in mortal danger. If we don't help them get to Switzerland, they will die!'

"The religious leader would not let up. 'What you are doing,' he said, 'is endangering this very village and the church itself! You must stop!'

"Pastor Trocmé was adamant: 'If we stop, many of them will starve to death and the others will be rounded up and killed. We cannot stop. We will not stop!'

"And then the Pastor did something amazing. He called the local church elders together and asked if they would accept his resignation. The council's vote was unanimous: *No!* It was a clear encouragement that Pastor Trocmé was to continue to follow Jesus, even if it meant disobeying the German occupiers, the French police, and even the leadership of his own denomination. They knew the teaching of the pastor – that the love of Jesus commanded them to love the stranger and the weak.

"It was a dangerous love, this love of Jesus. And it was a strange, strange situation. France, a supposedly 'Christian' country, had been invaded by Germany, another 'Christian' nation. The 'Christian' government, unchallenged by the church, was rounding up 'non-believers' and killing them.

"But in this one little village – a village of fewer than 5000 people, there was no betrayal. There was nothing official. There were no 'procedures'. But the truth is this, my friends: that after Magda Trocmé greeted that first refugee, no Chambonnais ever turned away someone who needed help. In spite of the fact that their own lives were in danger, that their own food supplies were running low, no Chambonnais ever denounced or betrayed a refugee. Le Chambon was a city of refuge for more than 5000 Jews – the village sheltered more foreigners than it had citizens!

"'How could they do this?' I see the question on your lips, Madam," the Frenchman said to Claire. "Because they listened to the Pastor's sermons. And the Pastor preached Jesus. And the pastor reminded them that they had been baptized. And if they saw themselves as baptized, there really was no choice. They had to follow Jesus."

At this point my friend could not help but interrupt. She said, "But how did they do it! Surely there was a cost!"

"Of course there was a cost!" the Frenchman replied. "Following Jesus is dangerous business. The Pastor and several others were arrested and often harassed. There were three deaths that I can tell you about. The Pastor's cousin, Daniel Trocmé, was arrested for aiding the Jews and ended up being gassed to death in a concentration camp in Germany. The town doctor, Roger Le Forestier, was shot by the secret police while he was on his way, strangely enough, to help injured Germans. They were sure he was going to help the foreigners.

"And there was another death during that difficult season: my faith died. You have not asked me my name. I will tell you now: my name is Jacques Trocmé. I am the son of Magda and André Trocmé. I was there.

"I saw it. I saw it all. I heard Father's sermons. I read the Gospels with him. I was hiding outside his door the terrible day when the leader of the church told him to stop helping the refugees. I wept when the Christians in other countries pretended it was not happening.

"I have heard people refer to what happened in Le Chambon as 'heroic.' Why? Why should following Jesus be considered heroic? Why should living out the practical implications of one's baptism be considered to be somehow remarkable?"

I noticed that the man had begun to weep, and as his voice trembled with emotion and memory, it grew louder and more strained. "There were hundreds of villages in France in the 1940's. There were hundreds of thousands of Christians. Yet there was only one Le Chambon. *Why?*"

He looked directly into our eyes and said again, "Why!?!" with a sound between a shout and a sob. He slapped his hand on the table and turned his head aside. The gentle hum of the coffee shop had stopped and all ears were turned towards our table. Aware of this, the Frenchman stood and said, "I will leave now. I have said too much."

We protested and asked him to sit and tell us more, but he refused. He said, "I hope I am a Christian, but do you know I have not been into a church since those days in Le Chambon?[3] I have come to agree with the Englishman, Chesterton, who said that 'the Christian ideal has not been tried and found wanting; it has been found difficult and left untried.'[4] It was tried, *mes amis*, in Le Chambon, but to my knowledge, never since. *Au revoir.*" And he raised his hand to us – almost as if to bless us – and walked to the door.

The coffee shop got back to normal. Claire remained seated across from me, but thankfully, she was silent for a few moments as I considered the awesome story that I had just heard. It occurred to me that the institutional Church is used to taking its time, has become adept at being measured, considering and contemplating and planning. But the people in Le Chambon did not have the luxury of "due time". They had to act in real time.[5] There was an urgency about their discipleship that I have never faced. I wondered what I would have done.

I was lost in my thoughts when I saw that my friend was standing to leave. She placed a ten-dollar bill on the table and said, "Do you see, Pastor Dave? The world is watching you and the rest of your church. I know you are baptized. The neighborhood knows you are baptized. Are you a follower of Jesus? Is your church a place of dangerous love?" She paused, and gazed into my eyes with an intensity that discomforted me. "I dare you to live like you believe it," she said. "If you do, then you might even see me

---

[3] While Jacques Trocmé did in fact leave the church following the events outlined herein, the interpretation of the reasons for his "loss" of faith are my own.

[4] "What's Wrong with the World," *Christianity Today*, Vol. 39, no. 1.

[5] This juxtaposition between "real time" and "due time" is explored by Hallie (p. 291), although his responses are different than mine.

drag myself into church one day. But unless the world sees you actually living like Jesus, nobody is going to pay any attention to the stories you tell about him."

And she walked out the door, leaving me with nothing but half a cup of coffee and my baptism with which to face the rest of the day.

Baruch Remembers
Luke 2:8-20, Matthew 2:1-18,
Habakkuk 3:16-19
Christmas 2001

Joseph? Hmmm. I
know a Joseph – he is a tailor
in Bethlehem. A carpenter?
No, I'm sorry. I don't…
Wait – wait! Do you mean a
man from Nazareth? A
carpenter who was here for
the census? He had a young
wife and a baby? Yes, I know the man. I have met him twice. The first
time I laid eyes on him, I kissed him. The second time, I tried to kill him…

No, I don't know what's become of him, or his family, for that
matter. But since it is a cold night, and because my sheep are all settled
down for the time being, I will tell you of those two meetings.

The first time I met him was on a night like this. It was cool and
crisp, and there wasn't a cloud in the sky. In fact, the stars shone so brightly
it seemed as if it were daylight. My brothers and I were out, as usual, with
the sheep. At this time of year, there is plenty of forage for them close by,
so there's no need for us to go far from home. In later months we're not so
lucky. But we were sitting out not doing much of anything – talking,
singing, staying close to the fire – when we saw something we'd never seen
before. The sky itself opened up and was a blaze of fire. And then I heard a
voice, and saw a figure – an angel – who talked about the birth of the
Messiah – the Savior.

I got up, and was transfixed by the messenger from God. He told
us that God's deliverer had come – the messiah for whom we had hoped for
so long! My brothers saw and heard it too, and then it was as if every star in
the sky became an angel. Never in my wildest dreams had I thought to see
such a thing. The messengers directed us to go into the village, and we
would there see the One who was born to be king.

That's when I found this Joseph. We simply left the sheep and
went directly to the village. We found the stable and there, in the manger,
lay the baby. He was just a baby. Nothing much to see, of course. We all
had babies. But then we talked with the man, Joseph. We told him what we
had seen – and he did not believe us at first! It was only when we described
for him the things the angel had said that he relented. And then he told us
what had happened to him, and how he in fact was a descendant of King
David. As we sat in the stable, we heard the marching of the Roman
soldiers in the streets. We saw the lights from Herod's palace. And we

celebrated – we celebrated the fact that God does move in our own time and in our own lives. It was a night like none I have ever known. I can tell you that when all the sheepskins were empty, I embraced this Joseph and kissed his cheeks, blessing him. Then we headed out to collect the sheep, as the sun was rising, and we were filled with hope and joy. We had seen – WE had seen – the deliverance of Israel!

It was maybe four or six months later that I saw him for the second time. I would guess that it's about five or six years back. It had been a dry winter, and we were forced to wander far from the village to find pasture for the flocks. We had been out to the east and were just coming back into the foothills of Judah – just coming into the areas that we normally frequent. In fact, we had just come into view of Herod's palace – the Herodian – that serves a vivid reminder that although we were almost home, our home was not at all free – that in spite of angels singing, there are tyrants and oppressors on the loose.

I don't know if you've ever been out much, but at night, around here, people don't usually move that much. As you can see tonight, there are a dozen or more watchfires amongst the various camps. If you stay long enough, you'll be able to tell the difference between the blazes of small groups of working men such as we and the campfires of the various traders who are heading up and down along the Via Maris – the Way of the Sea that leads into Egypt.

And if you have been out on nights like this, you know it's not uncommon to see caravans of traders circled for the night; groups of shepherds out on the hillside, and even the occasional band of soldiers settling into an encampment. But what you rarely see is a small, unarmed group of people walking in the dimness of the moonlight. When one of those people is a woman, you know that something is just not right.

We saw such a group that night, and invited them to share our supper and the warmth of our fire and rest in the night. The man didn't even acknowledge us, and made as if he would keep walking, but woman said that she needed food, and they stopped. When they came close to the fire, I saw that there were just the two of them, although the woman had a baby. When the man pulled back his hood, I recognized him as the one you call Joseph – the father we had seen in the barn. There was a glimmer of recognition in his eyes, and we hurried to call my brothers in with more wine so that we might enjoy our time with the young deliverer and his family – and find out what was causing them to move so secretly in the night.

As he ate hurriedly, Joseph described for us the visit of Wise Men from the East. Kings, he said, had come to pay homage to the boy that we had seen. At this, my younger brother Ehud burst in: "We saw them! Do you remember, Baruch? We saw the caravan as it went through the pass in the East some months ago!" And we began to chatter excitedly about what the visit of these Magi must mean for the future of Israel. But Joseph waved his hands for silence, and the terror and panic in his eyes were evident for the first time all evening.

He started, "I had a dream three nights ago…" But before he could finish his sentence my cousin Nathan gave a cry. "Baruch! Look – over there! Is that your child?" And I looked and in the darkness I could make out the figures of two or three young people from the village. One of them was my eldest child, a daughter, Miriam. She was in tears, and her clothing was torn and ragged. She rushed to me even as her cousins rushed to my brothers. "There has been terrible evil!" she said. "King Herod has sent his soldiers into Bethlehem. They went into each house, and if there was a boy of two years or younger, they killed him right there. In our home, we tried to hide the baby, but he cried out and was discovered. The soldiers killed him. Mother is home, covered in blood. You must come quickly, father!"

The sound of the crying around me let me know that my son was not the only one to die that night. Two of my brothers had lost their boys as well.

In my shock, I heard a different cry. It was the baby that the woman was holding. In a moment I knew – I knew! That this man's baby was the cause of death in Bethlehem. The man, Joseph, was looking at me with terror in his eyes. His wife was crying softly. And the baby – their baby – their safe, healthy, baby just sat there in her lap.

It was incredible. I had prayed – we all had prayed – for God to act. We all had prayed that Yahweh would come into history and show his saving power. And when Joseph's son had been born, it seemed like God was answering the prayer of generations. But now? Where was God now?

I threw myself into a rage and jumped onto the man. He did not defend himself as I rained down the blows upon his head. He had sat at my table and eaten my food – and yet it was because of him that my son lay dead. I wanted to kill him – truly, I did, for he had cost me my future.

My brothers pulled me back and let Joseph get off the ground. I simply collapsed. What should I do, I wondered. If I raised the alarm, then Herod's soldiers would find this boy and kill him, too. And I thought, why should one live and so many die? Wouldn't it be better for one to die that many would live?

I had half-decided to send my Miriam to the soldiers when the unexpected happened. The child's mother, still weeping, stood from her place at the fire and stooped low to me. She put her baby into my arms and asked, "Will the death of this baby save you? Will your pain be less if you kill him now?"

I was silent, and simply stared at the child. After a few moments, Joseph spoke. "He's not really my son, you know. You were the one who told me what the angels had said. Do you think that I wish this upon you? Do you think that I wish this upon her?" And he gestured to the child's mother. "If what the angels have said is true, then there is a promise. Tonight, I run towards Egypt. My wife and I are not carrying a baby, but a promise. Do what you will – but I can do no other." And with that he took the child, handed it to its mother, and they began to walk once more towards the south – to Egypt.

If there is one thing that makes us who we are, it is the fact that we are a people who will hold God to his promises. Yahweh is a God who is not detached, who is not remote. The God of Abraham, Isaac, and Jacob is a God who is active in the affairs of men. If God is choosing to act through a baby, then I will choose to believe – even when that means pain.

I remember the words of the prophet Habakkuk, who said,
I hear and I tremble within; my lips quiver at the sound.
Rottenness enters into my bones, and my steps tremble beneath me.
I wait quietly for the day of calamity to come upon the people who attack us.
Though the fig tree does not blossom, and no fruit is on the vines; though the produce of the olive fails and the fields yield no food; though the flock is cut off from the fold and there is no herd in the stalls, yet I will rejoice in the Lord: I will exult in the God of my salvation.
God, the Lord, is my strength.[6]

I have thought about that night time and time again. Each time I sit under these stars and look at the sky, do you think I do not wish to see the angels again? When I hear the children playing, do you think that I do not feel the pain of my son's absence? How can I not feel that? Of course I do. But I know that there is no pain I've felt that is not common to the rest of the world. My brothers have known grief. You have known pain. The call of God to his people is to be those who hope in the midst of tragedy. To hold onto the promise – the promise that tells us who we are.

Years ago, God said that he would send a savior, and that all who believe will find life in his name. In my own time, I have seen angels telling me that this savior has arrived. So tonight, in spite of the emptiness of my own heart, I will believe the angels. And I will pray for Joseph and his son. And I will pray for you, too, friend, that you might find the wholeness and the healing that God promises. Amen.

---

[6] Habakkuk 3:16-19a, NRSV

I Remember, and I Would Do It Again[7]
Matthew 2:1-12
Christmas 1999

The two young men walked quietly into the darkened house.
"Uncle? Uncle?" The taller man called softly as they entered.

There was no answer. They were sure that the old man had finally
died - that he had finally, it would seem, have gotten his wish. The men
went straight to the bedroom, expecting to find the worst, but to their
surprise and relief, it was empty. Even as they wondered where their uncle
had gone, they could not help but pause for a moment in this chamber. It
was perhaps the most incredible room they had ever been in - and each time
they came to this house, they would stop and investigate the treasures that
this room contained.

On the walls were many tapestries and hangings, richly interwoven
with silk and even gold threads. Feathers of a hundred colorful birds had
been fashioned into a cape that lay draped over a chair in the corner. There
must have been two dozen ceremonial cups and goblets scattered among the
shelves, many of them encrusted with a variety of jewels. And, of course,
there were the scrolls. Everywhere you looked, there were the writings.
Some of them were charts of the stars, others written in any one of ten
different languages, all filled with mysteries of the ages.

Astorius could not help but look at his older brother and say, "It's
incredible - it seems as if this room has never changed!"

Before the other man could reply, they heard a raspy voice calling.
"Mentar! Astorius! Is that you?"

"Coming, Uncle" the young men said as one, and hurried onto the
small balcony at the rear of the house. There they saw their uncle, looking
frail and weak, clutching a ragged blue cloth, looking heavenward.

It was not unusual for the old man to be in this position -- after all,
he was - or at least he had been - an astrologer. For years, he had followed
the stars in their courses. He had told the future by looking into the
mysteries of the heavens. All around Persia, it was said, that Balthazar was
the one to call if you needed to know the future. The relics in the bedroom
were all that was left of those days, however. He had suddenly stopped

---

[7] The title of this message is a quote from T. S. Eliot's "Journey of the Magi" (1927), which
serves as the inspiration for this story.

watching the heavens nearly twenty years ago. So perhaps it was unusual to find Balthazar out on the balcony, looking at the sky. What was even more unusual, however, was the fact that he had moved there by himself and that he had a light in his eyes like none his nephews had ever seen.

"Uncle, Uncle," sighed Mentar. "You are not well. Let me put you back to bed."

The old man simply shook his head and pressed the dusty cloth to his face and inhaled deeply. "I will stay here," he announced.

The young men didn't know what to do, so they sat on the floor and waited. As they watched, their uncle repeated his movements several times: he would hold the cloth, almost as if it had a medicine in it, and inhale slowly. After a few moments, Astorius said, "Uncle, your kerchief is dirty. I will find you a clean one."

"NO!" said Balthazar with a sharpness that surprised them all. "Listen to me - this fabric is the chief of all my treasures. Even now, you can go into the house and take what you want - only do not take my breath from me."

"But uncle," Mentar protested, "that's nothing but a rag. Surely the great Magi Balthazar needs silk next to his face!"

"You sit there, boys, and I will tell you the story of this, my most wonderful treasure. For I have seen the star again tonight - not the same star, mind you, but a star in the same place. I know that my own time is passing, and you should know what I know.

"It was the last journey that I undertook. It must be years - I don't know, twenty? - it seems a lifetime ago. I had been watching the skies, and a strange, new light appeared. Whereas many times before stars had come into my vision and had shown me something, this one was different. I knew that it meant something, but what?

"As I was puzzling one evening, my colleague Melchior arrived. He had journeyed three days to come to my home. He, too, had seen the star and was hoping that I knew what it meant. For nights we struggled, and finally decided that it was the star of a king - a king greater than we had ever known. It was Melchior's idea - how I wish it were my own, but it was Melchior who said, 'We must go and pay homage to this great king.'

"I agreed at once, of course, and we put together a caravan with spices and gold, and we began to travel west. Six days into the journey, we met another of our kind, one named Caspar. He, too, had seen the star, and had come to the same conclusion - it led to a king, a king who would be worshipped. Naturally, we fell in together.

"It was a hard journey. The weather was terrible, and the further we got from home, the worse the travel became. The servants became scared, and one by one they ran off into the night, sometimes stealing a camel, other times taking our money or food. The inhabitants of the cities through which we passed regarded us as a curiosity, and took advantage of our situation to overcharge us for even using their wells.

After three months, it was just the three of us, still following the star. We came into the land of Judea, and met with the governor there, but it was immediately apparent that he knew nothing of the star or of the king for whom it shone. In fact, that idiot could not even see the star when we took him outside of his own home and pointed to it. Here was Melchior, practically reading a scroll by the light that shone forth, and this barbarian who fancied himself a king could see nothing.

"We left as quickly as we could and followed the light to a village not many days away. Now, hear me, Mentar. Hear me, Astorius. I have said that the star seemed to blanket us with light. When we got to the village, it shone more like a torch, or like a sun-beam. It was, it seemed, barely in the heavens. It beckoned us, and so we followed, as in a trance. In fact, I was so intent on following the star that at one point I stumbled and before I knew what had happened, the camel had stepped on my arm and broken it.

"Earlier, that would have been enough to make me stop, but I could almost see into the heart of the star. It didn't matter. I was going to worship this king, even if I had to crawl on my knees.

"And then - well, then it seemed to stop. We were almost into the village, and we were beginning to look for a palace - and the star simply stopped. At first we kept going, thinking that we would discover a new road, but we left the light behind. We came back to the point where the star had stopped, and discovered that it had gone altogether. It just wasn't there any more.

"We sat by the road and wondered what this meant. In the months of travel and study, we had see the star increase and decrease. We had seen the buffoon of a king be unable to recognize the star. But always, always, we had seen and been able to follow. But now we were in the darkness - there was not even a moon.

"We sat in the darkness for nearly an hour. When we got up to move, my eye caught it. It was a dim light, to be sure, but it was a light. It was a cave - a cave just under the spot where the star had stopped. We hadn't seen it before because the star had blinded us. But in the dimness of the moonless night, the entry to the cave stood before us and beckoned us in.

"We entered and saw a peasant family - a mother, child, and father. I turned to go, thinking that we must have been mistaken, when Caspar fell to his knees. 'This is the one,' he said. 'This is the child who has the power of the star.' And Melchior was doing the same thing. And then in my heart, I, too, knew, that I was in the presence of a king. Not any kind of king, exactly, but clearly a person of majesty and power and holiness.

"The family was not surprised to see us, but when we got our gifts to present, they protested. The man said, 'See, strangers, we have nothing to offer you in return. Will you embarrass me in front of my family by offering us such wealth that we cannot repay?'

"We tried to tell the story of our journey, but when we started to talk about the star, the woman interrupted. 'It is enough,' she said. 'We know the star. We know who sent you.' And then it was like we were with family. The man drew water for our beasts, and set them to feed. We sat down, and that's when the woman noticed my broken arm. She took one of the rags in which the baby was wrapped and fashioned a sling for me. We slept - we slept like we hadn't slept in months - in the safety of that cave.

"The next day, the man told us strange stories of the child. We had thought that he was a king, but the man spoke of him as a deliverer. They said the baby's name: Jesus, or Yshua, which in their language means, "God will save".

"They told us of their God - a God who was a creator who loved his handiwork, and who sought to be in relationship with his people. They spoke of grace, hope, and joy. And they knew that this child was their God's doing.

"And I don't know even today if I dreamed it or if it happened, but I know that in the presence of that child there was grace, hope and joy. We rested together for two or three days, and they told us more of their God. They prayed for us, and then we parted ways. They were going south, they said, and we looked to the east.

"We didn't talk much on the way home. Caspar left us fairly soon, saying he had business somewhere else. And Melchior didn't talk at all. By the time I made it home, my arm had healed, but I couldn't throw this rag away. It was somehow a kind of proof that the trip had taken place, and that the baby had been born, and that there is a God who offers grace, and hope, and joy."

At this point, Balthazar stopped so long that his nephews began to wonder if he had fallen asleep. Just as Mentar was going to get up, the old man breathed in deeply through the fabric once more.

"Listen to me, children. My whole life, I've been a traveler. I know what it is to be a stranger - to travel a road and be unknown and even unwelcome. That's why this house has -- had -- always been so important to me.

"But something happened in that cave. I was not a stranger there. I was at ease. There, in my brokenness, my pain; there, looking at a mystery that I didn't understand - that is where I felt . . . where I felt the breath of heaven.

"And ever since the day I left that cave, I have been a stranger. It doesn't matter where I go, I am ill at ease. I gave up the arts when I returned home from that trip. I am no wise man. I am no king. I focused on my failures, or at least my weaknesses. The skies were dark to me.

"And then tonight, I heard the wind whispering out here. And I came out, and I see the star - I see a star, anyway - in the place where there was a star so many years ago. And tonight, tonight I can sense that grace, hope and joy right here. It's like this piece of cloth carries within it the breath of heaven that I sensed in the cave. The woman's child - his name was "God will save."

"Mentar, Astorius, the darkness is lifted. The baby is going to be a king - but a king unlike any king that you have ever seen. Listen to me: Do you see that star?

The young men indicated that they did, in fact, see a star.

"I remember that night. I remember, and I would do it again. I cannot. But you can. I want you to take everything that is in this home and sell it. Use the money that you receive and follow the star. It will not be an easy or a short journey. But use all that you have to follow that star and meet the king who is God will Save."

Astorius and Mentar started to argue with this kind of foolishness, but before they could speak, their aged uncle put the cloth to his face, drew in one last breath, and died. And, for the first time in their lives, they saw a smile on his face.

The next day, the young men did as their uncle had commanded. They sold everything and went on a journey to find and to worship the child who had been born a king. And from that day to this day, wise men and women have been doing the same thing. May the promise of such grace, hope, and joy fill us with such a hunger for the breath of heaven that we, too, will follow the star, even when, or perhaps especially when, it means taking a journey that changes us forever.

The Journey of the Magi
T. S. Eliot

This poem was written following Eliot's conversion to Christianity and confirmation in the Church of England in 1927. It was later published in *Ariel Poems* (Faber & Faber, London).

A cold coming we had of it,

Just the worst time of the year

For a journey, and such a long journey:

The ways deep and the weather sharp,

The very dead of winter.

And the camels galled, sore-footed, refractory,

Lying down in the melting snow.

There were times when we regretted

The summer palaces on slopes, the terraces,

And the silken girls bringing sherbet.

Then the camel men cursing and grumbling

And running away, and wanting their liquor and women,

And the night-fires going out, and the lack of shelters,

And the cities hostile and the towns unfriendly

And the villages dirty and charging high prices:

A hard time we had of it.

At the end we preferred to travel all night,

Sleeping in snatches,

With the voices singing in our ears, saying

That this was all folly.

Then at dawn we came down to a temperate valley,
Wet, below the snow line, smelling of vegetation;
With a running stream and a water mill beating the darkness,
And three trees on the low sky,
And an old white horse galloped away in the meadow.
Then we came to a tavern with vine-leaves over the lintel,
Six hands at an open door dicing for pieces of silver,
And feet kicking the empty wineskins.
But there was no information, and so we continued
And arrived at evening, not a moment too soon
Finding the place; it was (you may say) satisfactory.

All this was a long time ago, I remember,
And I would do it again, but set down
This set down
This: were we led all that way for
Birth or Death? There was a Birth, certainly,
We had evidence and no doubt. I had seen birth and death,
But had thought they were different; this Birth was
Hard and bitter agony for us, like Death, our death.
We returned to our places, these Kingdoms,
But no longer at ease here, in the old dispensation,
With an alien people clutching their gods.
I should be glad of another death.

John 1:1-14

1In the beginning was the Word, and the Word was with God, and the Word was God. 2He was with God in the beginning.

3Through him all things were made; without him nothing was made that has been made. 4In him was life, and that life was the light of men. 5The light shines in the darkness, but the darkness has not understood it.

6There came a man who was sent from God; his name was John. 7He came as a witness to testify concerning that light, so that through him all men might believe. 8He himself was not the light; he came only as a witness to the light. 9The true light that gives light to every man was coming into the world.

10He was in the world, and though the world was made through him, the world did not recognize him. 11He came to that which was his own, but his own did not receive him. 12Yet to all who received him, to those who believed in his name, he gave the right to become children of God—13children born not of natural descent, nor of human decision or a husband's will, but born of God.

14The Word became flesh and made his dwelling among us. We have seen his glory, the glory of the One and Only, who came from the Father, full of grace and truth.

The Spitting Image
Christmas 2008
John 1:1-14

If by chance you were to wander into the little town of Dominion, it would not leave much of an impression on you. There's just not too much "there" there, if you know what I mean. Down one of the side streets there's a small home with an oversized garage attached to it, and on the garage hangs a hand-painted sign that reads simply "Veronica's Wheel". If you're there on the right day, the lights in the garage will be on and you can enter; if you were to do so, you'd find that Veronica Adams is a potter, and the garage is her studio.

Two or three days a week, you can find Veronica sitting at her wheel, shaping lumps of clay into all manner of beautiful and useful vessels. If you were to watch her carefully, you'd notice that as she sits down, she always follows a little routine. She places a quantity of clay on the wheel, starts it spinning, and before she reaches for the sponge to moisten the surface of the clay, she spits in her hands and rubs them together. And if you were to ask her why she spits in her hands like that, well, most days she'd just smile and say, "oh, it's an old habit" and get to work looking for beauty in the clay.

But maybe – as she did with me – she'll stop the wheel, wash her hands, pour a mug of coffee that is both beautiful and delicious, and tell you a story.

Veronica's early childhood was unremarkable, so far as she could see. Her father was a letter carrier and her mother a nurse. Veronica was an only child, and she had some happy memories of her family – camping, holidays – you know, the usual.

All of "the usual" changed for Veronica when she was nine years old. She had been at a sleepover at a girlfriend's house when tragedy struck – a fire raced through her home, and not only destroyed the home, but killed both of her parents. She was an orphan.

It was terrible, of course. The initial shock, and the transitions that were to come. It was just terrible. But she was a nine year old girl, and nine year olds have a certain resiliency. She got through. She went to live with her aunt – her father's sister. She missed her parents, of course, but she also had what you might call a "normal" adolescence – she went to school, played in the band, had friends – in many ways she was a typical teenager.

The one thing that bothered Veronica, though, was the fact that this small town was filled with people who knew her whole story. From time to time, people would stop her in the market or at school and say something like, "You know, you really look like your mother…" or "Veronica, I'd say you are the spitting image of your father!" Veronica knew that these comments were intended to be kindnesses – she really did. But it was frustrating to her to think that she would never get to know her parents. She had memories, and a few photos given to her by others. And she heard stories, of course – she loved to hear the people talk about her father, who had a reputation for extraordinary honesty. Some of the "regulars" on his route had given him house keys when they were ill so that he could stop in and give them the mail and save them a few steps, especially in the winter. A photo of her mother was hanging in the pediatric wing of the local hospital, put there by some of the parents who had been especially grateful for the young nurse's outstanding ability to care for children who were terminally ill.

So Veronica was torn. On the one hand, it was nice to hear that she resembled her parents, and from what she knew, they sure seemed like amazing people. But it hurt that she would never know them, not much beyond the image that looked back at her from the mirror every day.

When she was nineteen, her grandmother – her mother's mother – passed away. Veronica went along to help clean out the home. Amid the cartons of Christmas decorations and out-of-date clothing, Veronica found a real treasure: a small box that contained a few of her mother's possessions, including a stack of letters that her father had written as well as the diary that her mother had kept while in nursing school. This was amazing!

For three days, Veronica stayed in her room and simply pored over the letters and the diary. She soaked in each word that her parents had committed to ink and paper. For the next three weeks, she set about the task of matching the dates on the letters with the dates in the diary, and she was able to read them almost as a conversation between these young lovers.

As she read and re-read these documents, she came to know her parents in a new light. Instead of seeing Hank the mailman and Gina the nurse, locked in time and space, she saw a young couple with dreams for the future. They had hoped to work in those jobs long enough to save some money to allow them to follow what they thought was the Lord's leading to open their home – or perhaps an even larger facility – to young people who had been abused or neglected – children who needed to know that they were precious to the Lord. She wasn't sure what to do with that information, exactly, but it meant something to have a more complete picture of her parents.

Veronica went to college and majored in the creative arts. When she was twenty-five, a trust fund matured, and she was able to open her own studio, and between the things that she sold on-line and in a few local outlets, she was able to support herself. She was pleased – not many people can say that they follow their dreams like that.

But she continued to hunger for a deeper connection with her parents. As she neared the age that they were when they died, it seemed as if her physical resemblance to them intensified.

One afternoon Veronica greeted a woman who had called looking for some special bridesmaid's gifts for her daughter's wedding. When the woman walked into the studio, though, she stopped dead in her tracks and did a "double-take". Finally, she said, "Your mother—was she a nurse?" Veronica nodded. The woman paused, seemingly uncertain about what to say next. Finally, Veronica spoke: "Did you know my mother?"

The woman sat down and said, "Yes, I did. More than twenty years ago, I had a baby – a son. He only lived about six months. He had a malignant brain tumor." The woman's voice was measured and the memory was clearly vivid. "He was too little to talk, and we knew that he was in great pain. Your mother – she was a young nurse then – she was the only one who could comfort him. She spent hours and hours just holding my son – when I was too tired, too depressed, too angry to do anything, your mother loved my son."

Veronica simply nodded – she had heard a few stories over the years. But the customer continued: "After the baby died, I gave up hope. My husband and I stopped doing much of anything. We were depressed…I don't know if you can imagine it. But your mother – first your mother, and then your father – they saved our lives. They came and cooked for us. They helped us care for our older son. Your father even helped my husband get a new job – we just couldn't stay in this town – we had to get away. Your father was so kind…"

Well, in the weeks that followed, the woman became a friend, and Veronica heard more of what had happened. She would visit the studio and they would talk about the details of the upcoming wedding for the woman's daughter, Regina. And the woman would tell Veronica stories about her mother and dad.

During one conversation, the woman said, "You know, when I first laid eyes on you, I recognized you as Gina's daughter. But I swear, Veronica, you are the spittin' image of your father."

Now, as I have mentioned, Veronica had heard all of this before. But there was something about the way that this woman said "spittin' image". She slurred it a little bit, and it sounded like "sprittin' image." Confused, Veronica asked her why she pronounced it this way. The woman laughed and said, "I guess that's the way that my grandfather always said it. He said that it meant 'spirit and image', and he used it to mean that a person resembled someone else in a way that more than merely physical." The woman continued, "You know, Veronica, you are the spirit *and* image of your parents. You don't only have their looks…you have their heart."

The spirit and image. Spitting image. Indeed.

Veronica turned that phrase over in her head for a week. It was delicious. It was delightful. It was like coming home after a long trip. She knew who she was – she was Veronica Adams. Hank and Gina's daughter, the spirit and image of her parents.

So if you ever visit Dominion, look for Veronica's Wheel. But make sure you look on Mondays, Tuesdays, or Saturdays. Those are the days that you can find her, sitting at her wheel, spitting into her hands as she asks God to use her to draw forth beauty and utility from the lump of clay that is before her. The shop is closed on Wednesday, Thursday, and Friday, though. On those days, you'll find Veronica on the grounds of the local Native American Indian reservation, where she spends her mornings conducting art therapy with children who have been traumatized and her afternoons teaching art in the church basement.

She knows. She gets it. Veronica Adams looks like her parents. But she has more than a passing resemblance: she has their spirit and image. She is a daughter. A wife. A mother. And she honors the life she has received by being the spitting image of the ones who gave it to her. And it is a good life.

The Greatest Gift of All[8]
A Children's Story for Christmas Morning
Or St. Nicholas' Day (December 6)
John 1:1-14

Today, I want to tell you a story about a boy who lived a long, long, long time ago - about 2 or 3 hundred years after Jesus was born. When the story starts, he's about as big as some of you - I think seven or eight. But just like you and me, he grew, and he became a man.

But anyway, the story begins when Nicky is about seven, and he was sitting in church one day when the people were talking about the Christmas story. One of the grown-ups was reading from the part where some men come to see the baby Jesus. Do you remember that part? Who were the men? What did they bring?

Well, Nicky thought this was great. He loved to hear the story about the three kings, and he asked his mother, "Who were those men?" And his mother didn't know what to say. Nicky said, "What were their names?" And his mother and father said they didn't know. They went to their minister, and Nicky asked again: "What were the names of the men who gave those presents to Jesus?"

And their minister told Nicky that nobody really knows who those men were. They just came and gave the presents to the baby and left. They never said who they were. "But why?" asked Nicky.

And then the minister got out the Bible and he read the very beginning of John's book to Nicky. It had a lot of hard ideas in it, and some big words, but there were some things that Nicky recognized. This is what their minister read to them:

The Word was first, the Word present to God, God present to the Word.
The Word was God, in readiness for God from day one.
Everything was created through him; nothing - not one thing!- came into
    existence without him.
What came into existence was Life, and the Life was Light to live by.

---

[8] This story was written using pieces of the Nicholas Legend gathered from Midred Luckhardt's *The Story Of St. Nicholas* (Abingdon, 1960), Duncan Royale's *The Santa Claus Book* (M.E. Duncan, 1983), Jeremy Seals' *Nicholas: The Epic Journey from Saint to Santa Claus* (Bloomsbury, 2005), Stiegemeyer and Ellison's *Saint Nicholas: The Real Story of the Christmas Legend* (2005 Concordia), and resources provided by the National Cathedral in Washington, DC.

The Life-Light blazed out of the darkness, and the darkness could not
   put it out. . . .
The Life-Light was the real thing: Every person entering Life he brings
   into the Light.
He was in the world, and the world was there through him, yet the world
   didn't even notice.
He came to his own people, but they didn't want him.
But whoever did want him, who believed he was who he claimed and
   would do what he said,
He made to be their true selves, their child of God selves.
The Word became flesh and blood, and moved into the neighborhood.
We saw the glory with our own eyes, the one-of-a-kind glory, like Father,
   like Son,
Generous inside and out, true from start to finish.[9]

   The minister explained to Nicky that one of the reasons that God
sent Jesus to us was so that people could know that we were God's special
children. That was a wonderful message, and the three kings, the wise men
who brought gifts to Jesus knew that Jesus was great. They brought him
presents to honor him, and to say thank-you to God for sending his son.
Their names weren't important, because Jesus was God's special gift to his
children.

   Well, Nicky thought this was <u>really</u> cool, and he decided that he
wanted to be like those three kings. And do you know what? He was.

   About four or five days later, Nicky was sitting by the street in front
of his house watching the smaller kids play. All of the children were
laughing and running - all except for little Anya. Anya was only three, and
she was crying by herself. Nicky went over to see what was wrong, and she
only cried more. But he sat and watched, and do you know what he saw?
He saw that all the other children had a toy or a ball, but Anya had none.
Her family was too poor. No wonder she was so sad.

   That night, Nicky asked his father to show him how to use the
special carving knife to make things out of wood. With his daddy's help,
Nicky made a small bird out of wood and he sneaked over to Anya's house
and left it by her door. What do you think happened the next day?

   All the children came out of their houses to play, and Anya found
the little toy. She asked all of the children who left it for her, but nobody
knew (except for Nicky, and he didn't say anything!). How do you think

---

[9] From John 1, in *The Message*

Nicky felt when he saw Anya playing with that bird? You know that he felt great! He felt just like one of those kings who had come to leave a present for baby Jesus.

Well, Nicky grew up, and every now and then, one of the poor children would find a carved bird, or maybe a rattle or set of jumping sticks by his window. Nobody ever knew where those toys came from - but I do!

One thing that I haven't told you yet is that Nicky's family was really rich, and they had more money than they needed. But they weren't always lucky. In fact, when Nicky was still a young man, both of his parents died, leaving him a very wealthy young man. But many of the families where he lived were so poor that they had nothing. And sometimes, after a person sold everything he had and was still poor, that person would have to sell himself or herself and become a slave - just so they wouldn't starve to death!

St. Nicholas and the Penniless Maidens by Gerard David, c. 1500

One night, when Nicky was grown, he was walking though his village and he heard a man crying. He went to the window of the man's house, and he heard that the man was actually praying. Nicholas could see that the man was very poor, and very sad. When he listened, he heard the man telling God that he was so poor that he was going to have to sell himself or one of his three daughters as a slave, just to make sure they didn't starve to death. Nicky was very sad when he heard this prayer, and he ran right home and found some money he had been saving. He went back to the window and listened to the man some more, and then he was very quiet and he dropped his sack of gold money through the window.

And do you know what happened? When that purse went through the window, it hit the shelf and bounced into a stocking. So the next morning, when the poor man and his three daughters were getting ready to go to the slave market, the oldest daughter reached for her stocking, found the bag of gold, and their family was saved!

Well, Nicky grew older, and he kept reading the stories about Jesus. He never forgot that Jesus came to remind us that we were all special, and to make things right between us and God. Everywhere he went, he told people about the love of God. When Nicky became a man, he decided that God wanted him to be a pastor and serve God in a church, where he could spend all of his time telling boys and girls, men and women about the love of God.

For the rest of his life, every time he got the chance Nicky used to walk through his neighborhood and listen for stories of people who were in trouble. He knew that God loves the poor, and that God doesn't want anyone to have to do something terrible like selling themselves as a slave. And whenever he went out, he usually managed to leave something for the poor children - some candy, or a toy that he had made. And sometimes he hid the things in the stockings or the shoes that the children had left sitting by their windows.

Well, do you think that Nicky was able to keep it a secret forever? No, of course not. Sometimes people saw what he was doing. What do you think they did when the saw him?

It's funny. Some people, when they saw Nicky giving things away, tried to tell on him. When the child came out and found the toy or the candy, those people would say, "Big deal! It's only Nicholas that left it (that's what his grown-up name was, 'Nicholas' - but his friends still called him "Nicky")." Those people seemed to like spoiling the surprise.

But a lot of people, when they saw what Nicky was doing, they came and spoke to him about it. They asked him why he left presents for poor people, and do you know what he told them? He always told them about the three kings who came to leave presents for Jesus, and how nobody knew their names. He told them that he left presents for people so that they would remember that God loves them, and that God wants to be their friend. And when Nicky told the people that, do you know what the people did? Some of them acted just like Nicky, and THEY went out and left presents for people and helped to take care of the poor, too.

I should tell you that it wasn't just the presents that Nicky was famous for. He came to be known as a man who knew right from wrong. People respected his views. Once, someone had hurt someone else very badly. The crowd in town found three strangers and figured that they had done it. Nicky, however, knew that the men were innocent. Just when the crowd was going to kill the men, Nicky stepped in and convinced them to stop. He saved their lives!

And this went on for a long time, until Nicky became a very old man. He had become a very rich and very important man, called a Bishop, in his town that was called Myra. People came from all over because they knew that Bishop Nicholas could help them. And he did.

Well, one sad day in the wintertime, Nicky was so old and so tired that he finally died. All of his friends, rich and poor, were very sad. They missed him a lot, and they wanted to remember him. So some of them got together and talked about it.

Somebody said, "We have to think of a way to say 'Thank You' to God for giving us someone as wonderful as Bishop Nicholas. What can we do that will show God how glad we are to have known him?"

One person said, "Remember how Nicholas used to tell us about the love of God? What if we built a big church and named it after him? Then everyone could know that God loves us."

Someone else was remembering the way that Nicky used to worry about all the children who were sick, and she said, "What if instead of building a church, we built a big hospital, where sick people could get better?"

A few of Nicky's other friends remembered how he had always tried to make people happy with the Joy of the Lord, and they suggested that they have a big party with lots of games and singing.

Well, they talked and talked, but finally they got the perfect idea for how to say "thank you" to God for Bishop Nicholas. One of Nicky's oldest friends remembered the story of the three kings who came to see Jesus and how they left without anyone knowing their names. And you know, that's what they did. All of Nicky's friends got together and on the night of Jesus' birth, they went through the town and left gifts for the children. And on Christmas day, the children in that neighborhood woke up and discovered that there were gifts for them. And because Nicky's friends didn't want anyone to know who left these gifts, whenever anyone asked about the presents, they always said, "Well, it must have been Bishop Nicholas - you know how much he loved children!" And ever since then, people have been leaving each other presents and remembering Nicky - only now we call him Saint Nicholas.

Maybe you found a gift this morning that was left for you by someone who didn't want you to forget that you are a very special child of God. Maybe you found some special gifts in a stocking at your house! There's someone who wants you to know that God sent Jesus into this world to be our savior and our friend, and that Jesus is the friend of every boy and girl, rich or poor, in the world. And because you know that, you can now act just like Nicky did.

Sometimes on Christmas people give each other little gifts of oranges. Doesn't that seem like a funny gift to give? It does, until you remember the story of Nicky. Do you remember how he dropped the bags of gold into the window? Ever since Nicky died, people give each other oranges to remind themselves of the gold that Nicky gave to the poor. This morning, I want to give you all an orange, and ask you to share it…and while you do, tell someone else about the real story of Christmas – about the boy who was the Son of God, and about the boy who spent his whole life remembering the three kings.

Santa Claus and St. Nicholas

Everybody loves Santa Claus.
He embodies holiday cheer, happiness, fun, and gifts—
warm happy aspects of the Christmas season.
How do Santa Claus and St. Nicholas differ?

Santa Claus belongs to childhood;
St. Nicholas models for all of life.

Santa Claus, as we know him, developed to boost
Christmas sales—
the commercial Christmas message;
St. Nicholas told the story of Christ and peace,
goodwill toward all—
the hope-filled Christmas message.

Santa Claus encourages consumption;
St. Nicholas encourages compassion.

Santa Claus appears each year to be seen and heard
for a short time;
St. Nicholas is part of the communion of saints,
surrounding us always with prayer and example.

Santa Claus flies through the air—from the North Pole;
St. Nicholas walked the earth—caring for those in need.

Santa Claus, for some, replaces the Babe of Bethlehem;
St. Nicholas, for all, points to the Babe of Bethlehem.

Santa Claus isn't bad;
St. Nicholas is just better.

—J. Rosenthal & C. Myers

Seeing Is Believing
Christmas 2009
John 1:1-14

Whenever Christmas rolls around, I think of Charles. Charles was a young man who lived down the street from our home on Whittier Avenue years ago.

Charles was a big boy – very large for his age. From infancy, it was apparent that there was something, well, *different* about Charles. I'm sure that the educators or specialists would be able to tell you the name of the syndrome or condition that affected Charles' journey through life, but I think you will know what I mean when I say that he was what my mother would have called "slow". He wasn't profoundly disabled, if by "disabled" one meant that the opportunity to live a healthy and vibrant life was not open to him. Maybe I can put it this way: when he was in school, he was always just about the brightest kid in any of the "special education" classes, but when he was with the "mainstream", he tended to fall behind pretty quickly.

Like a lot of big boys, Charles was not exactly the picture of grace, physically speaking. He was clumsy: he could be counted on to be the one to spill the red pop on your new carpet. When he set to a task he did so with determination, if not always precision. And the lack of grace seemed to extend into social interactions as well. He talked loudly – embarrassingly so, and always at inopportune times. He had a very rich and pleasant laugh, but he tended to laugh for about fifteen seconds too long, if you know what I mean. And he was a hugger – Lord, was that boy a hugger. He loved to hug people so much that, well, he didn't always hug the "right" people, and surely didn't always hug at the right times or even hug you in the right places. Yes, Charles could be awkward.

Well, let me be honest. He could be more than awkward. He could be irritating. More than one of us thought that life was usually a lot more efficient and predictable when Charles wasn't around.

But the thing is, despite of all his clumsiness and lack of social grace, Charles was an incredibly kind person. As awkward as he was, he was that *good*. He was joyful. And so even when I say that life was usually a lot more efficient and predictable when he wasn't around, I need to say emphatically that life was somehow much *better* when he *was* around.

One year – it must have been near Easter time…Palm Sunday, I believe… Charles would have been about sixteen, and he saw the younger kids joining the church. You remember – all those eleven and twelve year olds standing up in front of the congregation making their confirmation. That afternoon, Charles went home and announced to his mother that he, too, would like to join the congregation. And so the next year, Charles joined the confirmation class down at the old stone church – a huge hulking, clumsy seventeen year-old giant somehow trying to keep up with lithe and bouncing pre-teens. As in many churches, the process culminated with each member of the class having to write a "statement of faith" – a one or two page document wherein each young theologian would speak briefly as to his or her deepest opinions on the great theological questions, such as the Trinity, or the doctrine of baptism, or the nature of the atonement.

And I'm not sure whether it was because he didn't want to press Charles too hard, or because he didn't want to spend countless hours coaching Charles through the process, but that year the pastor announced that there was a new rule. Only new members under the age of 16 had to write a statement. Anyone over 16 participating in the class simply needed to present a paragraph entitled, "Who is Jesus?" The pastor – trying to be kind, I'm sure - suggested to Charles' mother that they spend a little time looking at the gospels.

And most of that class – eight weeks, if I remember correctly – most of that class was predictable and smooth. It was efficient and calm – maybe even boring. It was what we've come to value and expect in most churches. It was "nice".

But behind the scenes, Charles was doing his best to read the gospels – reading them far more eagerly than the pastor had expected. And he got to John's gospel, where he read,

> The Life-Light was the real thing: Every person entering Life he brings into Light. He was in the world, the world was there through him, and yet the world didn't even notice. He came to his own people, but they didn't want him. But whoever did want him, who believed he was who he claimed and would do what he said, He made to be their true selves, their child-of-God selves. These are the God-begotten, not blood-begotten, not flesh-begotten, not sex-begotten.
>
> The Word became flesh and blood, and moved into the neighborhood. We saw the glory with our own eyes, the one-of-a-kind glory, like Father, like Son, Generous inside and out, true from start to finish. (John 1:9-14, The Message)

And he couldn't get over the richness of that passage. Heck, John had basically done his assignment for him. Who was Jesus? Jesus was light. Jesus was life. Jesus was in the world – better yet, Jesus was in the neighborhood! And John said, "We saw the glory with our own eyes…"

Well, I mean to tell you that Charles latched onto those phrases the way a pit bull latches onto a soup bone. And this is what he thought: that in church people sure talked about Jesus a lot, but not very many people seemed to be actually looking for Him.

But John said that Jesus was the Word, and that the Word had moved into our neighborhood. And if Jesus was in our neighborhood, Charles thought, he wanted to find Him. He wanted to bring him to church.

Right about that time, a new family moved into the house next door to Charles' family. You're going to think I'm making this up, but this is it: the new occupants included a single mother whose first name was Mary, and her nine-year old son, Emanuel.

The coincidence was not lost on Charles, who became convinced that maybe this was the "moving into the neighborhood" that John talked about. So I'm here to tell you that every day, Charles was over at that house. He tried as hard as he could to befriend that boy and his mother…but, as I say, Charles was not the most graceful person God ever put on this earth. Charles' attempts at friendship suffered a major setback the day that Mary called next door and explained to Charles' mother that Charles had come over to see Emanuel with a bag of quarters, a stick of cinnamon, and a bottle of perfume. "He said he didn't have any gold, frankincense, or myrrh, and this would have to do," said Mary. "I'm sorry, but this is creeping me out."

Charles' mother mentioned this to Ben Nichols, who had been Charles' favorite Sunday School teacher, and Ben took Charles out to breakfast to talk things over. Ben asked about the gifts to little Emanuel, and Charles told him about the promise in John – that Jesus had moved into the neighborhood. And Ben and Charles re-read John 1 right there at the diner.

Although I wasn't there, when Ben told me about it, I could practically hear Charles' piercing voice in the din of the diner: "…*The Word became flesh and blood, and moved into the neighborhood. We saw the glory with our own eyes…*"

Ben asked, "Charles, from what you know of Jesus, would he make a fuss when he moved into a new neighborhood?" And Charles thought about it for a while, and he remembered the times where Jesus did a healing or performed some miracle and made people promise to be quiet about it.

And then Ben Nichols said something that makes him about the wisest man I know. He said, "Look, Charles, I think you are on to something here. I think that Jesus *has* moved into the neighborhood...and I think that we've all missed it. I don't know who he is. I don't know which house he lives in. Do you?"

And that question hatched what Charles came to think of as "the Plan." Because he didn't want to miss out on meeting Jesus, Charles met everyone. Because he didn't want to miss out on blessing Jesus, Charles blessed everyone. Four times that summer, Mary came home to find that someone had cut her grass already. Twice, Charles rode the bus three extra stops because Mrs. Williams had a doctor's appointment and she was a little shaky. All up and down the street, neighbors began to find home-grown tomatoes and peppers on their doorsteps.

And let's be honest, most of the time, there was no great mystery here. Like I've said, Charles was not exactly tactful or covert. If he saw you carrying groceries in from the car, well, you wouldn't be carrying them alone. But some of it was less obvious. On Thursdays, Charles took to getting up a little earlier and walking behind the garbage truck. After all, he thought, if the trash collectors knew that it was Jesus' house, they wouldn't have left such a mess in the alley.

But then something happened that was not a part of the Plan. I noticed it one especially cold morning in November. We'd gotten an early snow that year, and as I stood with my cup of coffee contemplating the dark street, I saw my neighbor – Johnson – going down the street and brushing everyone's car clean. Not long after that, the Elliots had a death in their family, and two casseroles and three gift cards showed up within a day – while Charles and his family were visiting relatives in Philadelphia.

I noticed it at church, too. Sundays got longer. Not because the preacher talked any more (no loss there!), but because people stayed after church to talk with each other. And, more importantly, to listen to each other. When people talked about "prayer concerns", you got the sense that they really expected you to pray about the things that were worrying them, or to rejoice in the things that made them happy.

About six months later, Charles and his family left Whittier Avenue. His father got a new job two or three hundred miles away. The last I heard from them, Charles had gotten a job as a greeter at a local restaurant. And about three weeks after they moved, the Frosts moved into their old place. Less than a month later, while Ed Frost was out walking his dog, he asked me about Whittier Avenue. "What's the deal here?" he said. "I mean, we just moved in, and we sure don't know anyone at all, but it seems like every

76

day someone is leaving us something from their garden. I've already been invited to the Johnson wedding, and three people have asked me to come to church with them."

You know, some people say that it's nothing much. It's just the way things should be, they say. It's just people being nice. It's just people being neighborly. Maybe. But I say it's more than that. I say that the world on Whittier Avenue started to change the day that one person started to expect that he would find Jesus in the neighborhood. And I don't know about you, but I have. I have seen it with my own eyes. Thanks be to God!

The Word Became Flesh

Reflection: The Word Became Flesh

The theological word for this season is INCARNATION. It comes from the Latin *incarnatio*, *in* meaning in and *caro* meaning flesh. In flesh. Enfleshed. To make real or provide with a body.

That's what Christmas is all about.

Interestingly enough, the word "incarnation" does not appear anywhere in the entire Bible. You could scan from Genesis to Revelation, and you wouldn't find "incarnation". Buy the biggest, fattest concordance you can – and it's not there. But *incarnation* is what the Bible is all about: God becoming one of us. God, enfleshed.

It's crazy. How can the all-powerful, creative life-force behind the entire universe show up in a BODY? Yet Jesus is just that, according to the teachings of the Church: "I believe in one Lord Jesus Christ, the only begotten Son of God, Begotten of the Father before all worlds; God of God, Light of Light, Very God, of Very God; begotten, not made, who was incarnate by the Holy Ghost of the Virgin Mary and was made man…" (Nicene Creed)

That is Jesus. He is God, incarnate. Enfleshed.

The Bible may not contain the word "incarnation", but it sure does teach it. Scripture says over and over again that YOU are the body of Christ. When you go to church this Christmas Eve, I beg you to contemplate the flickering light in your hand, and to consider the power of God in the flesh, and to know that you are being charged to go out and be Christ's hands and feet in this world. How will they know? You can't talk anyone into believing the incarnation of God in the person of Jesus of Nazareth. God, in a body? It's just crazy. You have to show them. You have to, well, *incarnate* it yourself. I can't do it for you. Everyone has to do it in their own way and in their own lives. God bless you – as you show God's presence in the world.

Philippians 2:1-11

1If you have any encouragement from being united with Christ, if any comfort from his love, if any fellowship with the Spirit, if any tenderness and compassion, 2then make my joy complete by being like-minded, having the same love, being one in spirit and purpose. 3Do nothing out of selfish ambition or vain conceit, but in humility consider others better than yourselves. 4Each of you should look not only to your own interests, but also to the interests of others.

5Your attitude should be the same as that of Christ Jesus:

6Who, being in very nature God,

did not consider equality with God something to be grasped,

7but made himself nothing,

taking the very nature of a servant,

being made in human likeness.

8And being found in appearance as a man,

he humbled himself and became obedient to death—even death on a cross!

9Therefore God exalted him to the highest place and gave him the name that is above every name,

10that at the name of Jesus every knee should bow,

in heaven and on earth and under the earth,

11and every tongue confess that Jesus Christ is Lord, to the glory of God the Father.

Hasn't Anybody Seen Jesus?
Philippians 2:1-11
Christmas 2004

When Earl Johnson turned his Ford minivan into the parking lot the morning of December 27, he saw something he hadn't seen in…well, he didn't know how long it had been since there was a line of people waiting to get into his store. To be fair, two people only barely qualifies as a line, and, well, one of the people in the line works as a cashier at Johnson's Gift and Variety Store…but a line is a line is a line.

The second person in line was Brianna Morgan, the eighteen-year-old girl who was clerking at Johnson's while trying to figure out what to do with the rest of her life. It was no surprise to see her out front. Earl Johnson figures that she's lost at least three keys to his store in the past eight months. But there in front of the "line" was Natasha Banks. Uh-oh. This didn't look good.

The last time he had seen Mrs. Banks was about a week ago, when he sold her a nativity set. About an hour after she left, he got a phone call. "Mr. Johnson! You've got to help me! I need Jesus!" was the voice on the other end. Once he got over the shock of hearing that, he realized that it was Mrs. Banks on the line. She said, "Do you remember that nativity set I just bought? Well I got home and went to set it up, but Jesus is missing. Do you understand me, Mr. Johnson? Missing! How can I have a nativity set with no Jesus?"

Earl had allowed as how that might be problematic, and he said he'd try to find the missing figurine. In the meantime, he thought the simplest thing might be for him to simply give her the Jesus carving from a similar set that he had in stock. To his surprise, though, both of the remaining nativity sets were missing the Jesus figure. "What the heck?" he thought. "Who steals Jesus?"

He remembered asking Brianna to try to track down the missing baby, but he didn't have high hopes. After all, he joked to himself, it took three wise men a couple of months to find the Son of God, and they'd had a star to guide them. Brianna couldn't even keep track of her own keys.

So that's what he'd been thinking when he pulled into his usual parking place. He wasn't looking forward to this. First, he'd have to deal with an unhappy customer. Then, he'd have to give Brianna another lecture about "How are we supposed to keep up with Wal-Mart when we have to spend all our money on locksmiths." Nope - this was not the way he thought he'd spend the first business day after Christmas.

So Earl Johnson was a little more than surprised when, upon walking closer to the store, he saw Mrs. Banks give Brianna an envelope, and then both women did a sort of a squealy-thing, and embraced. Whatever else might be going on, nobody was upset this morning.

As he unlocked the door, Mrs. Banks reached into a shopping bag and pulled out a finely arranged gift basket that appeared to be stuffed with the kinds of gourmet coffees and chocolates that Earl really enjoyed, yet never bought for himself. "Merry Christmas, Mr. Johnson!" she exclaimed. "I'm sorry this is late, but it's not really a Christmas gift. It's a thank-you present."

If Earl had been confused before, he was positively bamboozled now. "I'm -- I'm afraid you've lost me, Mrs. Banks," he said. "I don't recall doing anything special for you, other than losing Jesus last week."

"That's the best thing that's happened to me all year!" Natasha Banks exclaimed. "That's what I'm here to tell you!" And then she and Brianna did that squealy-thing again.

They walked into the store and Brianna said brightly, "Mr. Johnson, I think you're going to want to hear the whole story. Why don't you and Mrs. Banks go back to the break room while I get the store ready to open today."

Earl gave Brianna the look that he usually reserved for those times when his wife and daughter had the plan already made and he knew that there was no real choice involved. "That sounds fine, Brianna. Thank you. Mrs. Banks, would you like to join me?"

Mrs. Banks smiled and said, "Of course - as long as Brianna remembers to set aside those other nativity sets for me -"

"I'm sorry, Mrs. Banks," Earl said. "I thought I'd mentioned that those sets were missing Jesus, too."

"Oh, you mentioned it all right, " she smiled. "That's why I want them." And she walked to the break room in the rear of the store.

After they'd gotten seated, Natasha Banks unfurled the story that had carried her into the shopping plaza that morning.

"First if all, Mr. Johnson, I need to apologize for the way I treated you last week. I know you were doing your best, and all I could think about was that someone had gypped me out of the baby Jesus in that manger I bought. I'm ashamed when I think about what I said."

Earl assured her that dealing with dissatisfied customers was something he'd learned to do a long time ago, and before he could apologize again for the missing infant, Natasha continued her story.

"You may remember that I called you on Monday - the day I bought the set. Well, on Wednesday morning, I stopped by the Post Office to mail my Christmas cards. I was waiting in line, and then your helper, Brianna, came in right behind me. You'll never guess what she had!"

Earl didn't even try to guess.

"She showed me a crinkled-up piece of a newspaper from Bethlehem. Bethlehem - in Israel! You see, the nativity set that you sold me was carved in Bethlehem, and the men must have used this paper to wrap the set before they shipped it. Anyway, when you told Brianna to look for Jesus, she went all through the boxes and found nothing but these newspapers - English-Language newspapers printed in Bethlehem. And, well, you know how Brianna can get side-tracked sometimes..."

"Believe me, Mrs. Banks, I know *very* well how Brianna can get side-tracked!"

"Well, she got to reading this newspaper, and it talked about how a church in Bethlehem was being closed down because of the conflict between the Muslims and the Jews in the Holy Land. Evidently, there's some sort of a boundary wall that's going up over there, and while it's really cutting down on the number of suicide bombings in Israel, some of the Palestinian farmers are really having a rough time making ends meet. The article talked about how this church had decided to start making food available to anyone who needed it - Christian, Jew, or Muslim - because of the travel difficulty. Well, someone thought that was a bad idea, and the church got bombed. Brianna got so wrapped up in this that she decided not to buy anyone Christmas presents this year, but to send all of her gift money to the missionary who was overseeing the food distribution. She was at the Post Office to wire the funds to Israel. I couldn't believe this young woman responding to the world's situation like that. It was a real shock to me."

None of this really surprised Earl. He knew Brianna to be a good kid. A little impulsive, perhaps, but kind-hearted and generous. She loves the Lord. He was proud of her. But this wasn't the end of the story.

"When I left the Post Office, I had to go to the hospital. Nobody knows this, Mr. Johnson, but I needed to get a biopsy done on a lump I've discovered on my neck. I was pretty scared...and still am, to tell you the truth. Well, on my way into the hospital, I ran into Phil Terrance. Do you know Phil?"

Most of the people in town know Phil. Up until last summer, Phil had the kind of life most guys dream about - great job, loving wife, and their only child was the quarterback of the high school football team. But in September, the boy, Sean, was diagnosed with a rare liver disorder. They had tried everything at the hospital, but Sean died on December 12.

"I was surprised to see Phil going into the hospital, and so I asked him if everything was all right. He said that things were going along fine - he was just there to see a friend. Do you know what, Mr. Johnson? Phil Terrence goes into that hospital every day! It turns out that the kid that was in the bed next to Sean has cancer. He's only eight years old, and he took it real hard when Sean died. It looks like this little guy is going to pull through, but Phil goes in to see him and to pray with him every day, just to try to give him a lift. I don't know how he does it, myself."

"Well, having my biopsy done didn't seem like such a big deal after that. I was hardly thinking about myself anymore - just wondering about what Phil and his wife were going to be doing on the holiday. That must be so hard...but they're really dealing with it. They've got some faith, that family does..."

"Friday night I went to the midnight service, like I always do. I got there kind of late, and by the time I parked the car and got in the room, my family had gone clear up to the front to sit. The pastor was already talking, and there was no way I was going to traipse up that aisle in front of everyone. So I just sat down sort of quick next to old Mr. Peters."

"During the announcements, the Pastor told the congregation that the Hawkins boy - Ronald, I think his name was - was one of the soldiers killed in that attack in Iraq last week. I heard something, and there next to me Mr. Peters was weeping. He said he was all right, it's just that he was sick of the killing. He told me that he'd buried a brother in France during World War II and had lost a nephew in Vietnam. This old man was simply weeping at the tragedy of war - he was crying for his brother, for his friends, for the Hawkinses...He was crying for the world, really, I think."

The room was quiet for a moment, because now Mrs. Banks was crying herself. Earl offered a tissue, but she waved it away and said, "No - no. I'm getting to the good part." After a minute, she continued.

86

"So we get everybody home from church and I put the kids to bed and make some last-minute arrangements around the tree. My eye happened to catch the nativity I bought last week when it hit me."

"Do you remember the last thing I said to you last week, Mr. Johnson?"

Earl said that he remembered her calling and looking for the missing piece of the nativity set.

"That's not quite right," she said. "The last thing I said to you before I hung up the phone was, 'For crying out loud, Mr. Johnson, hasn't anybody seen Jesus?'"

"I sat down and I held that little empty manger, and I realized that of course Jesus isn't in the manger. Jesus refuses to be kept in a manger. He's not lost -- he's out on a mission! You searched the store, and I searched my house, and he's just not there...because he's in the middle of cluttered lives and fragile families."

"'Hasn't anybody seen Jesus?' I have, Mr. Johnson. I have. I saw him at the Post Office, mailing food to people who are starving. I saw him visiting a scared child in the hospital. I sat next to him while he cried over the horror of war."

"My whole life, I've been trying to keep things in order. Trying to keep Jesus in the manger. But look, Mr. Johnson, now I see. Jesus doesn't belong on a shelf, waiting to be dusted or displayed. Jesus is alive in me, Mr. Johnson! Jesus is working in some of the darkest corners of this globe. And I saw him. I saw him."

"So thank you, Mr. Johnson, for selling me that nativity set. And thank you, too, for selling me the other two that I think Brianna has wrapped up for me this morning. I can't wait to drop them off at the

Terrence's and the Peters'." Natasha Banks stood up and extended her hand. "Thank you again, Mr. Johnson. And merry Christmas!"

She shook his hand and left the small room. Earl sat there for a moment and tried to digest everything she had said. It was an amazing tale. Then he heard the front door open and close and saw that it was already 9:30 and time to open.

When he'd left home this morning, he was expecting to deal with the rush of post-holiday bargain-hunters. But when he left the break room, he wasn't looking for customers any more. He was looking for Jesus. And if he were here tonight, he'd tell you that that's made all the difference. He's found the truth: that once you look for Jesus, you discover that Jesus has been looking for you for a long time. That is the Good News that we hear at Christmas! God bless you.

Joey To The World
Christmas 2006
Luke 2:1-12, Philippians 2:1-11

Sometime around Thanksgiving, Joey Wright's mother said to her thirteen-year-old son, "You know, Joey, I haven't seen a Christmas list from you this year. What do you want?" Joey looked at his mother and said, "Um, mom, I don't think I want any presents this year. I've thought about it, and I have everything I need. Can I do something special for Christmas this year?"

"Joey, if it's about taking that trip to California to visit your uncle, well, you know we can't afford that kind of expense this year…"

"No, mom, that's not it at all," Joey interrupted. "I was wondering about doing something else. Do you remember that man who came to church last month and talked about the homeless people? I was thinking that maybe instead of me getting presents, we could take some money to that shelter he was talking about."

His mother smiled, and said, "All right, son, I'll make you a deal. You save some money, and at Christmas time I'll double whatever you have and we'll mail a check to the folks at the homeless shelter."

Although Joey knew something about saving money, he wasn't at all sure about sending checks anywhere. But since his mother was already on the way out the door, and since she had already basically agreed, he let it drop. And he started saving and planning.

It took about three weeks, but by the 22nd of December, Joey was sitting on top of $63. He had never in his life had so much money. He hadn't told anyone about his idea, but he got $20 from his grandmother for Christmas, like always. He shoveled snow a couple of times for the neighbors, and that was good for $14. He had skipped lunch three times a week at school, and that gave him another $11 and change. And he couldn't believe it when he found, down by the corner, a few crumpled-up bills that added up to $18. He had never held that much cash before. He thought about his mother's promise – to double it – but he never thought he'd have so much money. And he knew that she was always short on cash, and it didn't seem fair to him that she should have to double money that he found on the street. Plus, he had a plan.

He didn't want to send a check. He wasn't interested in mailing anything – he wanted to take something – he wanted to take himself! So that evening he got on the internet and found the address for the shelter. The next morning – it was a Tuesday – he walked out the door with his backpack and his books, as if it were simply another day at McWhertor Middle School. But instead of walking to school, he kept on going until he got to the bus stop. He wasn't sure exactly where the bus would take him, but he had an idea.

The plan would have gone all right, except he hadn't figured on rush hour traffic. The bus sat in a line of cars that stretched for miles. As they got closer to town, a woman got on the bus and sat next to him. This was a new and exciting adventure for Joey, and of course he wanted to share it. The woman who was with him was very interested in his story, and wanted to know how much money he had and where he was taking it. Joey carefully explained his plan to help the world, and she sure seemed fascinated by it. So fascinated, in fact, that she began to tell Joey that she was a friend of the man at the homeless shelter and she offered to simply take the money there herself. Joey thanked her, but said, "No, I need to go there myself. Do you want to go together?" The woman said she couldn't do that, but wondered if Joey might let her have $10 of the money so that she could take a taxi to an important meeting at a place where the bus line didn't run. She explained that her friend at the shelter had forgotten to give her the taxi fare last night, but that she was sure that the man would replace it when Joey got there. Joey wasn't sure about it, but ended up giving her the $10 because it sounded like she knew what she was talking about. Anyway, he still had $53 left.

The bus finally got into town and left Joey off in front of a big building that had lots of offices in it. He knew that the shelter was somewhere close, but he wasn't sure exactly where. A cold rain had started, and so he went into the office building. He saw a little boy sitting on a bench with his dad. The man looked angry, and the boy – who looked to be about six – was crying. He kept saying, "What about Santa, Dad? Couldn't we just ask Santa?"

Joey went to the family to see what was going on, and the man just looked away. The little boy, however, was eager to tell the story. It seems as though he was supposed to get glasses that would fix his one eye – it had some sort of problem that Joey didn't quite understand. The boy and his father thought that the glasses were all paid for, but there was something called a "co-pay" that cost $25 that they had to have before the boy could get his glasses. Since it was so close to Christmas, and since the dad had lost his job, they didn't have the money to buy the co-pay, so the little boy's eyes were still not right. The little boy wanted to ask Santa for the money.

Joey prayed about it for a moment, and then he took a ten dollar bill and three fives from his pocket and gave it to the boy and walked through the doorway before the boy's father knew what was going on.

He walked down the street a block or two, looking for the address of the homeless shelter. He couldn't quite get the numbering system down. He ducked into a Laundromat to get a better look at the paper out of the rain. He smoothed it on top of one of the dryers. Outside, he noticed a tiny old woman trying to carry three garbage bags of clothes inside. He dashed outside and helped her carry her things inside. She thanked him, and he helped her sort the things into various washers as he asked for advice as to how to get to the shelter. She looked with some concern at a boy so young who was asking about a homeless shelter, but he didn't say why he was anxious to get there.

Joey found that he liked talking to this woman – it was obvious that she was on a tight budget, but she gave him half of her sandwich and they split a can of pop. It was hot in the Laundromat, and before long he had taken off his sweatshirt and they were playing cards and talking as her items dried.

After a bit, he remembered his mission, and so he told his new friend, "Thanks for the sandwich, Mrs. S., but I'm going to get going." She allowed as to how her things were just about finished, too. While she started packing up her old garbage bags, he headed to the rear of the building for a quick stop in the men's room before going to the shelter. He was so anxious to deliver his $28 and save Christmas for some needy family.

When he came out of the restroom, the woman had left. The paper with the address for the shelter was still laying there, but his jacket and sweatshirt were gone! He thought back, and the only thing he could think of was that she had somehow gathered them up with her clothes by mistake. He panicked, and ran outside. Just as the icy blast hit him, the bus drove by. Joey looked up in time to see a little old lady smiling down at him from the window seat…it was Mrs. S. And she was gone. And so was his coat, his sweatshirt, and his $28.

He didn't know what to do! Now, he didn't have any money or a jacket. The only thing he could think to do was go to the shelter and see if they would let him use the phone to call his mother. He hated that idea, but it was all he could think of. As he walked down the street, the rain intensified, so that by the time he reached the shelter in the middle of the next block, he was soaked through.

He entered into a cold-looking lobby, and there was a security guard there. Joey explained his situation and the woman looked thoughtful and then picked up her walkie-talkie. As he waited, the enormity of his situation finally hit Joey: he had lost all of his money, he had lost his coat, and worst of all, he had lost his chance to help needy people at Christmas. It was the one thing he wanted to do – and he had blown it! He started to cry – he didn't want to, but he was so cold and so sad. It was then that the man Joey remembered from church came down. He took a look at Joey, smiled, put his arm around him, and led him to a kitchen area where there was some hot cocoa.

Joey blurted out the story as the man handed him a towel and listened to him. When he was all finished, the man stood up and said, "Joey, I'm touched and humbled by what you have done."

And Joey just cried again and said, "Don't you see? I didn't do anything? I lost everything! I'll never be able to make Christmas special to anyone!"

And the man just sat down and said, "Joey, don't you think like that. These people that you saw today, some of them you helped. And some of them might have taken advantage of you. And sometimes we just have accidents. But listen to me: you are a part of what God is doing in the world. In fact, Joey, you are what God is doing. Every day – not just Christmas – God is sending you into the world to look for someplace that needs his attention. And when you find that place, or that person, then you pray about it and see what God wants you to do about it."

Joey started to complain about Christmas again, but the man interrupted him. "Son, the world is full of people who want to do things on one day. We have something for today. We need people to be here – and all over the world – next week and next month. And not just here – wherever you are."

The man talked some more – he talked until Joey's mom came to pick Joey up. I'm not sure of everything that he said, but I know it had an impact. I know this, because I know Joey. All of this happened about 8 years ago, and Joey is now about 21 years old and a student at college. And every day, before he leaves his apartment, he sees a little sign taped above the mirror. It's a faded index card written by someone about thirteen years old, and scrawled on it are the words "Joey, to the world." It's the way that he remembers that every day God is sending him out to look for those who need a smile, a sandwich, or a friend. And most days, Joey comes back home thinking that perhaps God has given him more than he's given the world. It took him $63 and all day one December in 1998 to learn it, but he knows it now: he is Joey, to the world. And yes, the Lord has come!

What Do You Need To Know?
Philippians 2:1-11
Christmas 2000

It doesn't really look like much on the map, but Exeter is a small suburban community on the fringe of a large northeastern city. Well, actually, it doesn't really look like much in real life, either, to tell you the truth. It's the sort of community that really has no community, if you know what I mean. A collection of office buildings, a drive-through restaurant or two, a couple of hundred homes, and a school.

And there on what passes for the main street, Sinclair Avenue, is a modest three story brick building called "The Phillips Complex" which houses, among other things, the broadcast studios of WWXN, which bills itself as "the voice of truth in a Godless age". It turns out that the "voice of truth" is mostly long-distance here in Exeter, at least at WWXN, whose programming consists mainly of syndicated broadcasts of any number of conservative preachers from the Midwest and the South. There's a two hour Southern Gospel time slot on Saturday evenings, and a religious news-magazine on Sunday afternoons. The only really local programming offered at WWXN is provided by the owner of the station, who hosts a show called "Dr. Fran, the Bible Answer Man." Each weeknight from 7 – 10 p.m., listeners are welcome to phone and find the answers to their Bible questions.

You might perhaps forgive Mike Edwards for being less than thrilled with his job. Mike is a Studio Technician at WWXN, which means that he is in charge of lining up and playing the audio feed from the various syndicators. On many nights, he also is in charge of screening the calls to Dr. Fran's show.

Mike is not from Exeter, and doesn't intend to be there very long. He's been there for about four years so far. He'd wanted to go to college, but there was no money, so he headed for the city looking for work in electronics. He ended up in Exeter, working at WWXN, which was at least mildly surprising, as Mike claimed no faith at all.

Working with Dr. Fran, unfortunately, was not bringing Mike any closer to faith. He was looking for something *real*, and he wasn't finding it. A typical evening at the phones was something like this: He'd answer the call, and the voice on the other end would say, "Hi, this is Dave... I mean, Dale, and I have a question for Dr. Fran about relationships." Mike would write this on a card and hold it onto the window, and when Dr. Fran picked up that line, he'd boom out, "Hello, Brother Dale! You're on the air with Dr. Fran. What do you need to know?" That's how every caller was greeted, and Mike found it a little annoying that so many of the people who called used fake names, and that the things that they really "needed to know" were usually involving how to get over on someone else without missing out on too many blessings. For instance, "Rita" called and said that her daughter was asking way too many personal questions about Rita's current boyfriend, and wanted to know what the Bible had to say. Dr. Fran rifled through his Bible and threw out a couple of verses dealing with children respecting their parents and parents having total control over their children. It just didn't sound too great to Mike, who was more interested in trying to figure out why "Rita" and her daughter couldn't share values.

You see, to Mike, it seemed as though the show, and all of Christianity, really, sought to reduce the vast mysteries of life, the universe, and God into a series of handy little phrases and pithy sayings. Mike's discomfort grew when he discovered that the "Dr." in "Dr. Fran, the Bible Answer Man" wasn't really a degree, but rather an old nickname from High School.

But he stayed on, mostly because he was looking for something else, but not sure what he wanted, and at least it paid the bills while he was waiting.

And then there was the Christmas Eve when Dr. Fran came into the studio looking a little green. As a matter of fact, he looked terrible. He tried to say something about a stomach ache, but when Mike got within about eight feet, he could tell that the problem may have in fact started in his stomach, but it was not viral or bacteriological, but rather an issue of how many cups of eggnog the good "Dr" had ingested at his sister's holiday party.

I'm a little sad to tell you that Mike was less than charitable towards his boss that evening. He sort of enjoyed watching through the window and looking at Dr. Fran rifling through his card file of Bible topics, working hard to make sure that people knew the proper spelling of "frankincense" and what the bible had to say about in-laws that didn't give the kind of gifts that you were expecting. Mike chuckled a bit each time "You're on the air with Dr. Fran. What do you need to know?" came out – a little more slurred, each time, it seemed to him.

Mike was surprised, however, when he saw Dr. Fran motioning frantically for him to come into the studio just as one call ended. Mike had just put on a commercial for Walt Wade's full-service funeral chapel, and Fran was clearly in distress. Mike rushed in and Fran thrust the tattered index cards into his hands and said, "Look, I'm too sick to do this. We've got twenty-eight minutes left on the show. I can't throw up on the air. You do it."

Mike shook his head vigorously. "I don't know anything about the Bible," he said. "I can't". Dr. Fran said, "You have to. We can't do anything else for these last twenty-eight minutes." And he reached into his pocket and brought out two crisp new $100 bills. "Mr. Franklin told me you'd always wanted to be a radio host," the drunken man said.

As Mike sat there dumbfounded and surprised, he heard the Walt Wade commercial end and Dr. Fran leaned into the microphone even as he was getting out of the chair. He said breathily, "I've got a special treat for all of the faithful listeners tonight. We have a guest in the studio who's going to help you all out for the rest of the show. Please welcome . . . er. Mike . . . that is, . . . Elder Edwards, who's here to take care of you. Thank you Elder.." was all he could get out before he had to turn his head into the waste paper basket.

So this is how Mike Edwards began his broadcast career. He sat down in the chair, punched a flashing light, and took his first call. "Hi," he said. "I'm M... Elder Edwards, and, uh, what do you need to know?"

He took two calls that, mercifully, were easy enough. "Billy" wanted to know how far it was from Bethlehem to Jerusalem and Rachel wanted to know if the Bible really talked about a virgin birth. Using the index cards that Dr. Fran had highlighted, these were easy enough to deal with.

The next time he pressed the button and said, "What do you need to know?", he heard a silence and then a tired voice said, "It's Monique." Mike repeated his question, since he didn't really know what else to do. The caller said again, "It's Monique." Mike said abruptly, "Do you have a question, Monique? What do you need to know?"

And this is what she said. She said, "I need to know if there is hope for me. I need to know why I should bother with all of this. I need to know how to make sense of all of this going on now." And then Monique did something terrible. Monique began to cry.

Mike looked helplessly at Dr. Fran, who was busy re-decorating the corner of the office rug with various shades of "earth tones". He flipped through the cards and threw out a couple of verses. "The Psalms," he said, "say that our hope is in God. And Paul said, 'Faith, hope, and love abide, but the greatest of these is love.'"

But Monique didn't do what all the other callers did. She didn't say, "Thank you" and hang up. She said, "What is there for me? What can I do?" And for the next seven minutes, Monique cried and told her story. It turns out that she was eighteen years old. Her father had left six years ago. Her mother was stressed from dealing with Monique's two younger brothers, who were constantly in trouble at school. The landlord had threatened eviction and the gas was due to be shut off next week. And Monique had a dream of going to school to learn to be a nurse, but she was working for the local burger place.

I wish I could tell you that Mike had an answer for her, but he didn't. Instead, he let her talk, watching the clock, hoping against hope that she'd keep going until the top of the hour when "An Old Fashioned Southern Christmas" would begin and play for the remainder of the night. Unfortunately for him, however, she stopped talking with eight minutes left to go in the hour. And she said, "So that's what I need to know, Mr. Edward. What does the Bible have to say for me?"

And this is where the first step of this Christmas Miracle took place. Because right then, Mike Edwards said, "Monique, I don't know what to say. And I'll tell you that my name's not even 'Elder Edwards', it's just Mike. And I'm stumped."

And Monique thought for a moment, and then said, "Yeah, well, isn't everybody?" and then she hung up. Mike looked at the blinking lights in the studio for a few seconds, and then automatically grabbed the next line. "We've got time for one or two more calls," he said, looking dejectedly at the piles of index cards scattered over the floor. He punched line three and said, "So, what do you need to know?"

And this is where the second step of this Christmas Miracle took place, because "Lillian" from Edgemoor said, "I tell you what I need to know, Mr. Mike or whatever your name is. I need to know where this Monique girl is. Because she's in trouble and she needs someone." Mike explained that he was not able to give her phone number out, and had no way of knowing where she was. That did not deter Lillian. She said, "Well, Monique, I hope you're listening, because this is what you need to know. It's almost 10 o'clock now. At 11:00 I'm going to be at the church at the corner of Edgemoor and Riverdale Streets. And I want to help you, Monique. So I'll be there, wearing a red coat and a white hat. And I want you to come to church with me. And I want to help you. So Monique, if you're listening, I want you to come to church and so I'll know it's you, I want you to wear a little bow — you know those little things you put on the Christmas packages, you know, those little bows the card stores sell? I want you to wear a bow on your left breast, right over your heart, so's I'll know who you are."

Mike was silent, and then realized that Lillian had hung up. He threw a cassette in the machine which began to tell the listeners the wonders of the Fillmore Family Florists, and then went into the control room where, sixty seconds later, he connected the programming link that brought "An Old Fashioned Southern Christmas" to all of Exeter.

And then Mike Edwards took the new $100 bills out of his pocket and stuffed them into Dr. Fran's shirt pocket and said, "Merry Christmas, Boss," and left the building.

An hour later, a large woman stood on the steps of the church on the corner of Edgemoor and Riverdale Streets. She was wearing a red coat and a white hat. And this woman saw the third part of this Christmas miracle occur, because a young woman came up and shook her hand, and pointed to a red bow worn over her heart. As Lillian greeted her and they turned to walk into the church together, she was held up by another young woman, who shook her hand and pointed to a yellow bow she was wearing. While Lillian stood there trying to figure it out, two more women came up, and then a young man as well.

Do you know that by the time that congregation had sung the last verse of "O Come, All Ye Faithful" that the large woman in the white hat and red coat was surrounded by no less than 17 people, all wearing ribbons of one sort or another?

Well, by now you can probably guess the fourth part of this Christmas miracle. You see, as that service went on, the congregation sang, and they lit candles, and they prayed, and one thing became clear – very clear, at least to one of the young men in the third row from the back, left side.

Because as the minister stood up front and read from Philippians: Jesus Christ, who was God himself, became nothing and was found as a human being. He was a man, who lived a perfect life, and died on the cross – so that every man and woman, boy and girl, might know the real meaning and purpose of life.

And as he sat there and heard those words, he knew in his heart the truth. The real question is not, and never has been, "What do you need to know?" And, while "Who do you need to know" is a better question, perhaps the greatest question of all was answered that Christmas Eve. "Who knows you already – right now – where you are in your life – Who knows all that and loves you anyway?"

After the service, there was a small throng gathered around Lillian as she and a few of her friends hurriedly passed out a few items of food and began to take information for help with utilities and so on.

And here's a funny thing. Mike Edwards had gone to that church because he wanted to see Monique. He wanted to know what someone who needed that kind of help looked like. He felt like he just had to know. But he didn't go over to the crowd to find out. No, he just headed for the side door. But as he got his coat and instinctively looked in a mirror to adjust his hat, his eye drifted towards his chest, and it rested on the bright green bow that he was wearing over his heart. And then Mike Edwards knew what someone who needed the help of Jesus looked like.

And he smiled, and went on his way. But I am here to tell you that his path was never the same again. Thanks be to God!

One of Us
Philippians 2:1-11
Christmas 1995

     Kathy Guilder was a pretty unremarkable woman. Like many people who spend their time serving the public, she often faded into the background. Not many people knew the story of her life. No one that she had seen this day knew that she had become a widow at age 38, or that in the twelve years since then her daughter had grown up and moved away and was promising to write more often. No one asked about her car - a 1981 Ford something-or-other; she didn't really care for the car, and on nights like this it was pretty obvious that it didn't care much for her. No one knew that when she was younger, she had dreamed about being a newspaper reporter; not necessarily famous, maybe, but at least known. Respected. Liked. No one, including herself, would have guessed that she would have ended up here.

     "Here" was the somewhat deceptively named "Mountain Vue Diner". Kathy had been the all-night waitress in this little place on a flat stretch of nowhere off of Interstate 70 in Ohio for more than a decade now. There were no mountains in sight on even the clearest of days, and on this blizzard-like Christmas Eve, the best that Kathy could figure was that maybe her boss, Eddie, had gotten a good deal on a used sign someplace when he was looking to go into business.

     There wasn't much "town" around the diner, which survived mostly because of the highway traffic. The only other business within walking distance was a Gulf station that doubled as a stop for the Greyhound Bus Company.

     Of course, Kathy didn't think much about all of this as she went about her business that night. She did things as she often did - almost automatically - greeting the truckers, smiling at the children, and picking up after people as they left the Mountain Vue - people who were, perhaps, headed to sunnier, more hospitable rooms and lives.

     If you were watching her carefully, you might have noticed a slight change in her attitude when Billy came in. She didn't know Billy's complete name - nobody did. He was just Billy. He must have been a little touched, a little "slow" - at least he acted that way. If she were an educator, Kathy might have referred to Billy as "developmentally disabled", but she was not familiar with that term. She was very familiar with Billy, however. He had managed to get a job as a "mechanic's helper" at the Gulf station, and he was very proud of that position. He wore his navy blue wind-breaker with the Gulf logo and "Billy" emblazoned on it as if it were a medal of honor. If you were watching Kathy carefully, you might have noticed that her smile seemed to be a little deeper for Billy. She got his coffee a little faster, and when she said, "How are you doing?", she waited a half a second longer to hear his answer. Most people didn't notice, but maybe you would have.

One thing that you would have noticed - that everyone noticed - was the radio that Billy carried with him - everywhere. Billy didn't talk much, but if that radio was any indication, he listened a whole lot. As usual, he was sitting in the corner booth, fiddling with the dial. As Kathy wandered over to refill his coffee cup, she wondered what Billy was listening to tonight. She heard the strains of a soft ballad, as the woman's voice crooned,

What if God was one of us?

Just a slob like one of us

Just a stranger on the bus

Trying to make his way home

If God had a face what would it look like?

And would you want to see

If seeing meant that

you would have to believe

in things like heaven and in Jesus and the saints

and all the prophets...[10]

Kathy had a somewhat amused expression on her face as she walked away from Billy's table. It must be nice, she thought, it must be nice to be able to believe in a fantasy like that. It wasn't that Kathy didn't believe in God, exactly. It was more like they had had some sort of falling out over the years and they weren't exactly on speaking terms. And the lyrics to that song: "What if God was one of us? Just a slob like one of us - just a stranger on the bus, trying to make his way home . . ." She thought about that line as she eyed a trio of over-the-road truck drivers seated along the counter. "Talk about your slobs," she said to herself. "Sorry, fellas, I can't go for a God who looks or acts anything like you..."

---

[10] Bazilian, E. (1995), "One of Us" on J. Osborne's *Relish* (Island/Mercury records), 1995.

No, Kathy had been the victim of slobs too many times in her life to want to have too awfully much to do with a God who might or might not be a slob like one of us. That's one of the reasons she was here now. This was a nice place, a safe place, but also her place. She was in charge here, on the midnight shift. People came in and needed something, and she gave it to them. She didn't need them; no, it was the reverse.

Kathy was jolted from her thoughts by a blast of frozen air. She turned around to see a young family, with what looked to be a mother, a father, a very young son, and a baby. She showed them to a booth and offered warm drinks to the parents. The little boy appeared to be scared, and wouldn't even look at Kathy. She would have continued to try, but she noticed Billy off in the corner, waving his mug like a lunatic, yelling for coffee. Kathy took the pot and went to settle Billy down.

Evidently, he had given up on music and was now listening to a church service of some sort.

"Hey, keep it down, will ya Billy?" she said over the din of some congregation's attempt at 'O Come, All Ye Faithful.' "With tips like mine, I can't afford to be offending any atheists, OK?"

When she got back to the counter, she set the coffee pot down and reached into her apron. Her hands rested on the candy cane that one of her earlier customers had left for her. She looked at the little boy in the booth, and decided to give it another try. She walked over with her order pad in one hand and the candy cane in the other. She held it out. "Here you go, champ," She said. "Would you like a treat that Santa left here for you?"

The little boy looked confused. He started to reach for the cane, but pulled his hand back. Kathy offered again. Then the boy leaned to his father and whispered, "Daddy, I want to talk to her, but I need to know: Is she one of us?"

The father and mother began to laugh. "Yes, yes, Joshua, she is one of us." They must have noticed Kathy's perplexed look, because the mother continued, "We've been waiting and waiting for the bus at the gas station. He's never ridden the bus like this, and we didn't want to disturb the other passengers, so we told him he was only allowed to speak with one of us until we got to his Grandfather's house." She turned to her son and said again. "Sure, Joshua, she's one of us."

Kathy held out the candy cane and proceeded to take their order. She laughed and smiled, but was already beginning to turn this over and over in her mind. By the time she had reached the order shelf, she absentmindedly handed the ticket over to Alex, the cook. But she was struck by what this child had said.

"Is she one of us?" Kathy reflected on this. Was she? Who was Kathy Guilder, really? She came into the Mountain Vue every night wearing a name tag and a smile - but who knew her? She had spent ten years of her life being polite to everyone, but really being loved by no one. At this instant, it seemed to her as though she had hidden from all the real moments of life behind a plaid skirt, crazy hours, and a pot of decaf coffee. And now a three-year old boy had called her on it. In the end analysis, didn't Kathy Guilder really, finally want to be one of us?

In the midst of this intense reflection, the background drone of Billy's radio suddenly broke into her thoughts. He must have still been listening to the same station, because it sounded a lot like church:

The pastor was evidently reading the Bible – it sure sounded like the Good Book, at any rate.

In your lives you must think and act like Christ Jesus.

Christ himself was like God in everything.

But he did not think that being equal with God was something to be used for his own benefit.

But he gave up his place with God and made himself nothing.

He was born as a man

and became like a servant.

And when he was living as a man,

he humbled himself and was fully obedient to God,

even when that caused his death—death on a cross.

So God raised him to the highest place.

God made his name greater than every other name

so that every knee will bow to the name of Jesus—

everyone in heaven, on earth, and under the earth.

And everyone will confess that Jesus Christ is Lord

and bring glory to God the Father.[11]

---

[11] Philippians 2:5-11, NCV

In one of those moments of recognition that come along only once or twice in a lifetime, Kathy Guilder knew that those words were for her. She hadn't realized it before, of course, but now it seemed as though her constant prayer had been for God to like her, to become like her. And through the accident of a battered old radio tuned in by an illiterate man-boy, Kathy Guilder figured it out. God had become one of us.

She thought again about the song that Billy had listened to earlier. She glanced at the truckers seated at the counter; at the young parents trying to coax little Joshua into eating his green beans before his cranberry sauce; at Billy, still sipping coffee and listening to the radio, and she thought, God did become one of us. And he was a slob like us - but the real purpose of this was not so much so that God could somehow be just like us, but to demonstrate to us that somehow, he had made us to be just like him. And maybe that idea that she had given up on too many Christmas eves ago to keep track of, that idea that said that maybe Jesus was some<u>one</u>, not just an idea or a concept or a fantasy.

Maybe nobody else in the Mountain Vue Diner noticed a change in Kathy Guilder that night. If you had been there, you might have thought that her smile was a little more real; that her eyes seemed a little more eager to look at you, that there was some sort of music in her voice.

Billy was surprised to see that she gave him a second piece of pie for free and offered him a ride home when her shift was over. And after she dropped Billy off at his sister's' place in the trailer park, she got back on the highway to head for her own home. As she turned on the radio, her hands rolled back and forth on the dial for no reason in particular. And then she heard it again:

If God had a name what would it be?

And would you call it to his face?

If you were faced with him

In all his glory

What would you ask if you had just one question?

What if God was one of us?

Just a slob like one of us

Just a stranger on the bus

Trying to make his way home[12]

---

[12] Bazilian, E. (1995),"One of Us" on J. Osborne's *Relish* (Island/Mercury records), 1995.

And when she got home, instead of collapsing into bed that Christmas morning as she usually did after work, Kathy Guilder did something she had not done in a long time. She went deep into her basement and found her Nativity set. She set up the crooked barn, complete with its three-legged cow, powder-blue Mary, stoic-looking Joseph, and the cracked little manger with the shape of an infant in it.

And as Kathy Guilder looked at that crèche in the light of the rising sun, a tear rolled down her cheek. As she beheld that plaster infant, she whispered, "You're one of us. . . I'm one of us . . ." And she was right.

Isaiah 11:1-9

1 A shoot will come up from the stump of Jesse;
        from his roots a Branch will bear fruit.

2 The Spirit of the LORD will rest on him—
        the Spirit of wisdom and of understanding,
        the Spirit of counsel and of power,
        the Spirit of knowledge and of the fear of the LORD -

3 and he will delight in the fear of the LORD.
        He will not judge by what he sees with his eyes,
        or decide by what he hears with his ears;

4 but with righteousness he will judge the needy,
        with justice he will give decisions for the poor of the earth.
        He will strike the earth with the rod of his mouth;
        with the breath of his lips he will slay the wicked.

5 Righteousness will be his belt
        and faithfulness the sash around his waist.

6 The wolf will live with the lamb,
        the leopard will lie down with the goat,
        the calf and the lion and the yearling together;
        and a little child will lead them.

7 The cow will feed with the bear,
        their young will lie down together,
        and the lion will eat straw like the ox.

8 The infant will play near the hole of the cobra,
        and the young child put his hand into the viper's nest.

9 They will neither harm nor destroy
        on all my holy mountain,
        for the earth will be full of the knowledge of the LORD
        as the waters cover the sea.

I Will Hold My Candle
Isaiah 11:1-9
Christmas 2002

He always was - and, I suppose, always will be my hero. My grandfather. I guess I always felt close to him - I'm even named for him. Edward John. To make things simple, the whole family's always called me John - except for Pap. He called me Eddie, and I loved him.

He was born in Scotland, and had a tough, tough life early on. He came to America after World War I and settled down here with some of his other relatives. He married my Gram, and became a well-respected member of the community. It always seemed to me as if he knew everybody in town - and he probably did. He ran the only hardware store for miles around, and it was well known that if you needed a hard-to-find item, Ed would take care of you. He was funny, gentle, smart - he was my hero. I wanted to be him.

There was only one thing about Pap I didn't understand. Everyone else in the family went to church, but not him. And on Christmas, when people came from all over to be together, we went to the candlelight service together. And my Pap - my funny, gentle, Pap - well, not only did he not come to church with us, but it's the only time I've ever seen him make fun of my Gram. He would stay home and drink beer all night on Christmas Eve, and when we got home from church he'd be drunk - and angry! Every year, it was as if someone had gotten hold of the Pap that I knew and replaced him with a bitter old man. When I got old enough to understand a little bit about what was going on, I asked my Gram. She just shushed me and said that I wouldn't understand. She said it was because of the war, and that he would get better in a few days.

On Christmas Eve of 1965, something amazing happened. We all went over to Pap's house for dinner, like usual, and there was the old man wearing a suit and tie! He grinned and said that he was coming to church with us. I was 14 at the time, and had never seen him so excited.

We got to the church and everything went like it always did. There were the little kids in bathrobes acting out the story. And then we sang "Silent Night" and lit each other's candles. But when I reached over to light Pap's candle, I saw that he was crying. Not only that, he was singing in another language! "Stille Nacht! Heil'ge Nacht! Alles schläft; einsam wacht…"

After we came home, I asked Pap why he came to church with us. And he told me a story I've never forgotten. He said that when he was 18 he went into the Army back in Scotland in order to earn some money and help out at home. By the time he was 22, in 1914, he was a corporal in the Second Scots Guards, stationed in the trenches in Northern France. He talked about being scared to death by all the stories he'd heard about the Germans - he didn't trust them, he said, and he knew that they'd slit his throat as soon as say "hello".

On Christmas Eve his unit received orders from HQ at St. Omer, stating that the enemy was planning a holiday attack and to be extra vigilant. At 8:30 on Christmas day, he looked out and saw four Germans coming across the battlefield. His captain sent Pap and another fellow out - unarmed - to make sure that the Germans weren't going to cross the line. It turns out that the enemy carried a few tins of meat and a small barrel of beer. They wanted a Christmas truce!

Pap said that it took a while, but the beer helped things out and that by lunchtime, both sets of trenches were pretty well emptied of soldiers. At first, they buried the dead and cleaned out their trenches, but towards the middle of the afternoon, a fellow from Glasgow showed up with a soccer ball. An impromptu game broke out, with the Germans playing the Scotsmen. Afterwards, there was more beer, and the men sang Christmas carols together for hours. Pap said that they almost forgot that there was a war on as they told stories and even showed each other photos from home.

Just after midnight, there was an order from his Captain to return to the trenches. When the men were all back in the hole, the Captain fired three shots into the air. From across the field, the German commander did the same thing. The war was on again.

"Fancy that, Eddie," Pap said to me. "Here's the German, shaking my hand as if he were trying to smash my fingers, offering me cigars and a pint of beer - and then a few hours later, trying to put a hole in me headgear! It just didn't make sense to me at all. I had begun to believe that if in fact we were all Christians, then we'd work things out and go home. But before I knew it, I was burying my mates and trying to save my own skin."

It seemed as though Pap had a lot of hope - but that hope turned to anger. He reasoned that if the story of Christmas were true, then it should make a difference in the ways that we treat each other. But since they spent the next three years trying to kill each other, then the story couldn't be true. My Pap told me that as far as he was concerned, there was no such thing as peace on earth, good will towards men. It was just a lie, a hoax, invented to make people feel better. That's why he got drunk every Christmas, he said. He couldn't get that feeling of betrayal or disappointment out of his mind.

But in the summer of 1964, something amazing happened. My Pap got a letter from Europe. It was from a man named Johannes Niemann in Germany. And in the letter was a photograph with four or five soldiers holding a soccer ball. On the back was a note: "Christmas Truce, 1914. Fritz beats Tommy, three goals to two."

It turns out that Niemann had taken the photo on that Christmas Day, and somehow had tracked my Pap all the way to Pittsburgh. Moreover, Niemann asked my Pap if they could meet. Well, Gram had been after Pap to take a vacation, and so they did. They went to France in December of 1964, and there, along with a few of the other soldiers, they had a sort of "50th Anniversary Reunion". Niemann had been one of the first Germans out of the trenches, and he and Pap spent a lot of time talking about the War and how their lives had been affected. And Niemann talked with Pap about God. He told Pap that he was a believer in Jesus Christ.

"Now you're talking nonsense, Niemann!" my Pap roared. "How can you believe in a fairy tale like that? Don't you remember that we were trying to kill each other? That if someone asked you what you wanted for New Year's 1915 you'd have probably asked for my head on a platter? And I'd have wanted yours? We talked about religion all day that Christmas, but it was obvious on the 26th that there was nothing to it. It's a lie, Niemann, a lie."

"You see, Edward," the German replied, "I remember very well. There's not a day that goes by that I don't thank God for that Christmas

Truce. For you, that day has become some sort of a wall - it stands between you and faith. It's an obstacle for you to overcome. But for me, it's different. That day has always been a window - it has let me see the power of God at work.

"When that day dawned - on Christmas morning 1914 - we were at our worst. Men from all over the world - strangers with no reason to hate - were trying to exterminate each other. But even in the hell of those frozen trenches, the power of God's love broke through enough to give us a glimpse of what could be. Do you remember the Bible, Edward? Do you remember what it says in Isaiah? 'The wolf will dwell with the lamb...the cow and the bear shall feed...they shall not hurt or destroy in all my holy mountain, for the earth shall be full of the knowledge of the Lord as the waters cover the sea...' That's what our God is doing, Edward. It will come. I know it will come. I've seen it through a window - and I know it is happening. I want to be a part of it - and I want you to be a part of it, too."

And so it was in a little village in France that my Pap went to church for the first time in half a century. And it was a church filled with Germans and Scotsmen who had, at one point, sworn to kill each other - but on that night in 1964, they shared the light of Christ.

Pap said to me that Christmas Eve a year later - 1965 - "Eddie, did you see what it was like at church tonight? Did you see how everyone was holding candles and their faces looked a little different? Did you notice that there was some sort of a glow? Now imagine, Eddie, what it would be like if folks looked like that without the candles? - If we looked like that all the time? That's what I think the song means when it says, "Silent night, Holy night, Son of God, Love's pure light Radiant beams from thy holy face, with the dawn of redeeming grace..." Jesus is like that all the time, Eddie. The light just comes from him.

"Eddie," my Pap said, "I want you to think of these Christmas Eve services as a window in your life. For a long time, I didn't even bother looking because my heart was so closed. I know that most of your life isn't full of that kind of beauty or warmth, Eddie. But it should be. It should be. And God intends it to be."

He got quiet for a while, and I didn't know what to say. Then he reached into his pocket and brought out a little box that he had clearly wrapped himself. "Go ahead, son. Open it," he ordered me.

I had never in my life received a gift just from Pap. It was always on Christmas or my birthday, and it was always from Pap and Gram. But there were the two of us sitting in the kitchen, and I unwrapped this little box. Inside I found a stumpy little candle - maybe three inches long.

Pap smiled and told me that it was the candle that Niemann had given him in France the year before. And then he took my hands in his and he said, "Eddie, you can't do it by yourself. Life hurts sometimes. It hurts a lot. But you can remember the way that it's supposed to be. And you can hold your candle, Eddie. You can hold your candle."

And every Christmas since then I've carried that candle in my pocket. I haven't missed a service, and neither has the candle.

On Christmas Eve in 1982 I was on my way out the door to the midnight service. I got a call from my mother. My Pap had died that evening. I wanted to go home right away, but my wife reminded me that I was to sing the solo in church. Silent Night. And so I went to the service, and I sang Silent Night. And I sang it in German. And I rejoiced that my Pap was finally able to see the whole picture - not just through a window.

And so I'm here tonight. And I've got Pap's candle in my pocket. If it looked stumpy and shabby in 1965, you can imagine that it looks pretty beat by now. But I'll finger it in my pocket when we sing *Silent Night*. And I'll pray that just as the soft wax melts with the approach of heat and flame, that the hardness, coldness, or bitterness in your heart might melt into the warmth of this room.

It's not surprising that men want to kill each other. It's not surprising that we claim to know the truth, and then want to do unspeakable things. But what is amazing to me is that God would love us enough to want to do something about it.

I have a grand-daughter. Her name is Johanna. She's twelve years old, and I love her deeply. And she doesn't know it yet, but after church the two of us are going to sit at my kitchen table. And I'm going to give her a little box that I've wrapped myself. Inside the box will be a stumpy old candle, a tattered photo of a few muddy soldiers holding a soccer ball, and a small Bible.

I hope she likes it. More than that, I hope she lives it.[13]

---

[13] The Christmas Truce of 1914 is a well-documented occurrence. While this story is a work of fiction, some of the names, locations, and quotes were borrowed from research done by Mr. Tom Morgan. More information can be found on his web site at http://www.fylde.demon.co.uk/xmas.htm

Afterword...on Holding Candles on Christmas Eve

As we celebrate Christmas, we affirm an ancient truth: that Jesus of Nazareth is the image – the Spirit and Image – of God the Father. The Good News of Christmas is that in Jesus, we have the right to become children of God. As Eugene Peterson translates John 1:12-13,

> The Life-Light was the real thing: Every person entering Life he brings into Light. He was in the world, the world was there through him, and yet the world didn't even notice. He came to his own people, but they didn't want him. But whoever did want him, who believed he was who he claimed and would do what he said, He made to be their true selves, their child-of-God selves. (From *The Message*)

Beloved, who is God calling you to be? You are his precious son, his beloved daughter. I know that there are times when we can be tempted to believe that God is unknowable – that God is too distant. That we have moved too far away to ever connect again.

And yet, you have a love letter – the Bible – to read. A diary – the Book itself – to reacquaint you with the Lord. At this time of year, we each hold a candle to remind ourselves of the light that is here, and the light that we have shared in the year that has passed. But what is God calling you to in the future – in the days yet to come? My Christmas prayer for you is that you will discover his spirit and image at work in you...and that you will claim that spirit and image and allow it to produce great fruit in your own life.

The world knows that there was a baby born in Bethlehem. I do not think that I'm telling you anything this season when I tell you that Mary and Joseph had a baby. You know. Your neighbors know. Everybody knows.

So what?

Isaiah foresees a day when those in the darkness will see great light...when those under oppression will know freedom...when those accustomed to warfare and bloodshed will know peace. Can you foresee such a day? Perhaps more importantly, when your neighbors look into your life, can they foresee such a day?

The wise men came to see the baby. We know that part of the story. We love that part of the story. But when they left, they went home by a different way. That is, they were changed by their time with the Christ child.

What will you do when Christmas is over? I'll be in worship. You see, I'm trying to follow Jesus. It's not heroic. It's not remarkable. It's just what I'm supposed to do, that's all. If you want to follow Jesus, too, then I hope that you'll show up for worship. This week, and next Sunday, and the Sunday after that. In real time, I'm going to try to be **for** Jesus. I hope that you'll worship, because I'm pretty sure I can't follow alone. And maybe if we follow, the people whose lives seem to be dark might have some light and know that because we are **for** Jesus, we are **for** them, too. So I'll take my candle on Christmas Eve and hope that somehow my holding that light will make the world a better place for someone else and that together we will find the Light to whom all these candles point – Jesus Christ.

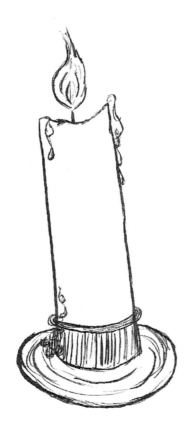